Praise for

BEYOND THE BUBBLE

"James Laxer has warned for years about the dangers of Canada's reliance on digging stuff out of the ground for foreign multinationals. He has been proven 100 per cent right by this latest and most spectacular economic crisis. His new book offers both penetrating critique and hopeful vision, and will be invaluable for Canadians struggling to build a better alternative."

— JIM STANFORD,
    Economist, Canadian Auto Workers, and author of *Economics for Everyone*

"This book offers solid evidence to refute the claims of those who insist that the current crisis is a temporary aberration in the economic cycle. It provides a powerful argument against those who are determined to put the system that caused the crisis back on track."

— JULIE GUARD,
    Associate Professor, Labour Studies, University of Manitoba, and editor of *Bankruptcies and Bailouts*

BEYOND THE

JAMES LAXER

BUBBLE

IMAGINING

A NEW

CANADIAN

ECONOMY

BETWEEN THE LINES
TORONTO

Beyond the Bubble: Imagining a New Canadian Economy
© 2009 by James Laxer

First published in 2009 by
Between the Lines
720 Bathurst Street, Suite #404
Toronto, Ontario M5S 2R4
Canada
1-800-718-7201
www.btlbooks.com

Every reasonable effort has been made to identify copyright holders.
Between the Lines would be pleased to have any errors or omissions
brought to its attention.

Library and Archives Canada Cataloguing in Publication

Laxer, James, 1941–
     Beyond the bubble : imagining a new Canadian economy / James Laxer.

Includes index.
ISBN 978-1-897071-55-7

1. Canada—Economic conditions—21st century.
2. Financial crises—Canada.   3. Globalization—Economic aspects. I. Title.

HC115.L395 2009   330.971'073   C2009-904222-3

Cover and text design: Gordon Robertson
Cover images: Shutterstock/Zacarias Pereira da Mata (industrial plant);
Shutterstock/1971yes (train); Shutterstock/xello (wind turbine);
Shutterstock/Radu Razvan (crosswalk); Shutterstock/Chen Ping Hung (flag)

Printed in Canada

Between the Lines gratefully acknowledges assistance for its publishing
activities from the Canada Council for the Arts, the Ontario Arts Council,
the Government of Ontario through the Ontario Book Publishers Tax Credit
program and through the Ontario Book Initiative, and the Government of
Canada through the Book Publishing Industry Development Program.

To the memory of Betty Price

CONTENTS

ACKNOWLEDGEMENTS

I am grateful to those at Between the Lines who worked with me on this project, in particular Amanda Crocker, Paula Brill, and Anjula Gogia.

Once again it was a pleasure to work with Rob Clarke, who did a fine edit of the manuscript.

Thanks to Daniel Grigsby for his research.

I am indebted to my spouse, Sandy, for her supportive presence while this book was being written.

J. L.

Chapter One

THE PASSING OF A WORLD AGE

———————

WE LIVE IN A TIME when technology and science have given people in rich countries the sense that, serious crises aside, things will go on as before; and that life may even improve if technology, science, and common sense are permitted to have their way.

For Canadians, who last saw their world torn apart in the 1940s—when they paid in blood with tens of thousands of soldiers killed—the past sixty years have been a relatively comfortable time. These decades, to be sure, have seen booms and recessions, natural disasters, human tragedies (such as the Air India bombing in 1985), the ugly loss of Canadian lives in Afghanistan, and the near division of the country in the Quebec referendum of 1995. But on the whole Canadians have been traversing one of the sunny uplands of history. For many of us this experience has provided the bearings for navigating the world.

But that world ended with the Great Crash in the autumn of 2008. Now it is time for us to acquire new bearings.

———————

The ending of a world age is something that happens more often than Canadians might generally think. While history has seen long periods of time in which life went on much as before and the great questions appeared to have been answered—the Roman Empire, for instance, during the second and third centuries A.D.—shock and transformation have been the regular accompaniments of human existence. Think of the fall of Carthage or the peoples of the Americas undergoing European conquest, or a young African boy or girl of the seventeenth century being brutally kidnapped and walked across the land to a slave ship bound for America, and you are on the way to conceiving of human existence as rife with swift change and destruction.

The age that ended in the autumn of 2008 was the American-centred age of globalization. That age had been a long time in the making. It took shape as a consequence of the interactions of forces of different durations. A central narrative in its construction was capitalism, combined with technology and science. Another narrative, closely associated with the first, was that of the rise of the United States and the American Empire to the zenith of global power, an achievement fully realized in the decades following the Second World War and consummated in supposed triumph with the collapse of the Soviet Union and its empire between 1989 and 1991. A third narrative, more limited in time, was that of the methods and practices of capitalism over the past thirty years, a time of global markets, deregulation, and neo-liberal ideology.

Not without an element of perverse humour in recent decades has been the launching on university campuses around the world of schools of business dedicated to training business executives, economists, and accountants imbued with the propositions of neo-liberalism. These propositions have played a not insignificant role in driving the world economy over the precipice. The hundreds of thousands of graduates of these business schools must now make their way in the world equipped with notions about economics that have as little explanatory value as Ptolemaic astronomy, Thomist theology, or King Canute's ideas about the workings of the tides.

While human beings are adaptive creatures—otherwise we would not have survived—we also have a remarkable capacity for rigidity and stubbornness, and a ferocious attachment to ideas that are no longer useful. One of the benefits, perhaps dubious, of civilization is that—granted a sufficient surplus for some to live off the labour of others—institutions, organizations, temples, churches, and political parties devoted to keeping alive useless and counterproductive schools of thought can exist. They can even thrive. During difficult times the attraction to the occult, to the reassurance of fundamentalist simplicities, and to wacky new age fantasies is great.

The pull to the irrational can also be strong in the political sphere. Take, for instance, the case of the Republican Party in the United States. After that party led the United States into unsustainable current-account and government deficits, wars that became quagmires, and the ballooning of the housing bubble that has now burst, one might have anticipated reflection and rethinking among its influential leaders.

Exactly the opposite has occurred. Talk-radio powerhouse Rush Limbaugh, a man who proudly denies that human activities have caused global warming, has become the party's leading figure. In his bombastic, bullying manner, he is unashamed to proclaim that he hopes President Barack Obama fails. Limbaugh and less extreme Republican leaders have responded to the global financial crisis with a return to the old verities. Instead of generating stimulus to offset the descent into depression—through direct government spending on infrastructure, on transit systems, on refitting homes for energy efficiency, or on education and health care—the Republicans favour tax cuts and cuts to government programs: the very recipe that fostered the economic crisis in the first place. Small government remains their cherished ideal, even though it was the Republicans who insisted on gigantic military budgets, trillion-dollar wars, and an agenda that made the super rich grow richer while the rest of the population faced rising debt and income stagnation. The Republicans contributed greatly to breaking the system that made their backers wealthy and helped ring down the curtain on a world age. This monumental failure, however, has not prevented the Republicans from calling for more of what did not work.

For their part, Canadian Conservatives, convinced that Canada and the United States were on the best possible course—that of a free market only lightly regulated—had no idea that an economic crisis was about to strike in the autumn of 2008. When Conservative Prime Minister Stephen Harper and Finance Minister Jim Flaherty travelled the road that began with them insisting that Canada would experience no deficit, only to arrive not many months later at the admission that there would be a deficit of at least $50 billion, they were not dissimulating. They just did not have a clue.

Both in the United States and Canada, the political right was blind-sided by the onset of the crash of 2008. Very few of them saw it coming. American Republicans and Canadian Conservatives saw themselves as competent managers of an economic engine in which the market was ever freer to operate without the constraints of government intervention. President George W. Bush was being sincere when he expressed his conviction right up until the moment when the financial meltdown struck in September 2008 that the fundamentals of the U.S. economy were sound. In Canada both Prime Minister Harper and Finance Minister Flaherty shared Bush's outlook: the economy was essentially fine.

Then it all came crashing down. Humpty Dumpty had a great fall. But the onset and consequences of the crash of 2008 and the changing political economy of the world that we live in are just one side of the story. The other side, just as important, is represented by the possibilities that this experience raises for socially fairer and more effective economic approaches in Canada and throughout the world. Although these subjects are intimately related, they are also different. My hope is that a compelling objective analysis of the first will help lead to an aspirational case being made for what I conceive of as a better future.

Can Humpty Dumpty be put back together again, and should we try? Or can we reconstruct the Canadian and the global economies to make the next global age fairer to the majority of people—as the age that has ended was not?

PART ONE

Anatomy of the Crash

Chapter Two

ONSET OF THE CRASH

PLENTY OF WARNING SIGNS indicated that the crash of 2008 was coming. Some of them flashed during the several months prior to the great financial meltdown that commenced in September 2008, and some of them were there for those prepared to notice them for years prior to the crash.

Notwithstanding the signs of an approaching catastrophe, the political and corporate powers that be insisted right up until Lehman Brothers filed for bankruptcy on September 15, 2008, that the economy was fundamentally sound.[1]

On August 9, 2008, with the stock market off its highs and turbulent, and with mortgage foreclosures skyrocketing, President George W. Bush called a press conference at which he declared, "The American economy is the envy of the world, and we need to keep it that way. . . . The fundamentals of our economy are strong . . . job creation is strong. Real after-tax wages are on the rise. Inflation is low."

Having delivered his anodyne message, the president headed off to Kennebunkport, Maine, and from there to Crawford, Texas, for a holiday.

On September 16, the day after the Dow Jones Industrial Average fell five hundred points, John McCain, the Arizona Senator who was the Republican Party's presidential candidate, also declared that the U.S. economy was "fundamentally sound." That day the lead editorial of *The New York Times* took aim at McCain: "Had he missed the collapse of Lehman Brothers or the sale of Merrill Lynch. . . . Did he not notice the agonies of the American International Group? Was he unaware of the impending layoffs of tens of thousands of Wall Street employees on top of the growing numbers of unemployed workers throughout the United States?"[2]

There was nothing remarkable about Bush and McCain insisting on the sound fundamentals of the U.S. economy. As president, Bush was not only defending his own record, but also sending out signals that he thought would bolster investors and help prevent collapse. McCain, though he portrayed himself as a maverick, was well aware that as the Republican candidate he would suffer from the growing conviction among Americans that his party had led the country into economic disaster.

Both because they have faith in the system they are directing and because they believe that expressions of confidence beget confidence, those at the helm are wont to assure investors and the general public that all is well. Some eighty years earlier, on December 4, 1928, President Calvin Coolidge, famed for his assertion that "the business of America is business," delivered his last State of the Union message to the U.S. Congress. He declared, "No Congress of the United States ever assembled, on surveying the state of the

Union, has met with a more pleasing prospect than that which appears at the present time. In the domestic field there is tranquility and contentment . . . and the highest record of years of prosperity." If that was not enough, he expressed the view that Americans could "regard the present with satisfaction and anticipate the future with optimism."[3] Just ten months later the stock market crash would usher in the decade of the Great Depression.

What is apparent from the cases of 1929 and 2008 is that those who have a huge stake in the economic system, whether as corporate executives or as political leaders, have a poor track record when it comes to foreseeing serious problems on the economic horizon. Those who benefit most from the system are overwhelmingly inclined to pay attention to positive indicators while ignoring the warning signs.

For its part, the Bush administration was deeply invested in the conviction that expanding home ownership in the United States was not just a key to increasing prosperity, but crucial in buttressing America as a market-driven society with less reliance on government. In addition, business interests, which were among Bush's biggest donors, had much to gain from the administration's home-ownership strategy.

Earlier, on October 15, 2002, President Bush had showed how he connected American well-being and home ownership when he stated, "We can put light where there's darkness, and hope where there's despondency in this country. And part of it is working together as a nation to encourage folks to own their own home." Bush and his closest political partners were convinced that extending home ownership to African Americans and Hispanics would help expand the Republican Party's appeal in these communities.[4]

The problem was that with house prices rising while incomes of the average American were not, to increase the number of home-owners the Bush administration favoured a loose regulatory system that could only encourage lax lending standards. The sub-prime lending market—lending mortgage money to people who were unlikely to have the means to repay it—was profitable enough as long as house prices continued to rise. If borrowers could not meet their mortgage payments, the lender could foreclose and sell the house for a higher price. Once house prices stopped rising, how-ever, and began to fall, as they did in the United States in 2007, the whole system worked in reverse. Then foreclosure meant seizing an asset that was falling in price and becoming ever more difficult to resell. Falling prices also meant that people in a house that could be subject to foreclosure had far less reason to try to avoid this outcome. By summer 2007 the foreclosure crisis was highly visi-ble. Sub-prime mortgages and toxic lending had become part of the public dialogue.

It is not that the administration had no warning that a foreclo-sure crisis, with implications for financial institutions, was in the offing. The administration preferred to run the risk because of what it saw as the benefits of the policy. Home ownership was on the rise, and homeowners were able to borrow money to make other pur-chases based on the equity they had in their houses.

As for the problem of the housing bubble, Lawrence B. Lind-say, Bush's first chief economics advisor, acknowledged: "No one wanted to stop that bubble. It would have conflicted with the pres-ident's own policies."[5]

When the foreclosure crisis hit financial institutions, the mem-bers of the administration that had helped create the problem were stunned at what had happened. On September 18, 2008, the president met in the White House with Ben Bernanke, chairman of the Federal Reserve Board, Treasury Secretary Henry Paulson Jr., and other economic advisors. Later a participant in that meeting remarked that the briefings "scared the hell out of everybody."[6]

A few days earlier Lehman Brothers had gone under, driven out of business by its holdings of worthless mortgages. Around the same time Merrill Lynch had been acquired by the Bank of America in a sale designed to prevent the global financial services firm from expiring. On September 16 the president had decided to extend U.S.$85 billion to American International Group (AIG). So central was AIG to the financing of failing mortgages that its failure would have dragged down a long list of other firms.

As Bush learned at the September meeting, credit markets had frozen. Financial institutions would not lend money. All at once the administration was forced to face an unmistakable fact: without urgent steps to pump liquidity back into the system and to start banks lending money again, businesses in every sector, lacking the normal credit on which they relied, would be unable to function. The political leadership of the United States was realizing that the country, indeed the world, faced the most severe financial crisis since 1929.

At that point the stock market crash had only begun. During the first eight trading days of October 2008, the Dow Jones Industrial Average (DJIA) dropped 2,399.47 points, or 22.11 per cent. The downward run began on Wednesday, October 1, with a small market slide of 19.59 points, followed the next day by a decline of 348.22 points and a further decline the following day of 157.47 points. The downward momentum continued on Monday, October 6, with a decline of 369.88 points, followed the next day by a loss of 508.39 points. The last three days of the trading week saw further declines.

On the following Monday the Dow Jones rebounded sharply with a gain of 936.91 points, only to have most of this momentum lost on Wednesday, when it fell 733.08 points.[7]

Many small investors not used to the brutality of the stock market crash continued to trust in the bromides dispensed by their brokers, financial advisors, acquaintances, and the media. The first of these shopworn pieces of advice is that investors, having been hit by the nasty plunge in the value of their stocks, should not sell stocks that have lost value. That way, they have been repeatedly told, they will not benefit from the rise in prices when they come, as they are sure to do. In the case of the 1987 market crash, which did not lead to a general economic downturn, stock prices quickly recovered. In that instance the general advice that one should stay in the market did make sense. But following the great crash of 1929 the Dow did not return to pre-crash levels until the autumn of 1954: a quarter of a century is a long time to wait.

The general advice to ride out a stock market crash, then, is not terribly useful. What matters is the specific nature of the financial and stock market crisis and whether it is related to a broader economic meltdown, as occurred in the case of the 1929 market crash and the subsequent Great Depression.

As in the case of the great crash of 1929, the demise of the speculative housing market and the plunge of the stock market in 2008 were not particular episodes that could be dealt with on their own. They ignited a far wider conflagration, a general economic crisis. A crucial element in that crisis was the widening in the income gap between the rich and the rest of the population, much as was the case in the late 1920s. Over the past thirty years the income and wealth gaps in the economically advanced countries have widened to a chasm. Here is a telling example: in recent years the relative income gap in the United States between the rich and the rest is wider than at any time since 1928 (the eve of the Great Depression.) In 2005, while the total reported income in the United States grew by nearly 9 per cent, the average incomes for those in the bottom 90 per cent of income earners actually declined slightly, by U.S.$172 or 0.6 per cent. The top 300,000 income earners took home a total remuneration that was nearly equivalent to the combined incomes of the bottom 150 million Americans. The privileged 300,000, per person, received 440 times as much as the average person in the bottom 150 million—the gap between the two cohorts having nearly doubled since 1980. In 2005 the top 10 per cent of U.S. income earners took home 48.5 per cent of all reported income, compared with roughly 33 per cent in the late 1970s. The all-time peak for the top 10 per cent was 49.3 per cent in 1928. In 2005 the top 1 per cent took home 21.8 per cent of reported income, more than double their share of income in 1980. In 1928 the top 1 per cent peaked in its share of income at 23.9 per cent. In 2005 the top tenth of 1 per cent reported an average income of U.S.$5.6 million, and the top hundredth of 1 per cent an average income of U.S.$25.7 million. The word "reported" is important. The U.S. Internal Revenue Service (IRS) has indicated that it can accurately tax 99 per cent of income from wages, but that it is only able to tax about 70 per cent of business and investment income, most of which goes to upper income earners.[8] What this means is that the IRS does not really know how much business and investment income is being earned in the United States. The consequence is that the real income gap is much greater than reported.

Compared to the lives of the rich and the super rich, the lives of ordinary people were growing ever more uncertain on the eve of the crash. Most people were on an economic treadmill, precariously attempting to make ends meet and to ward off the growing danger of crippling indebtedness.

Just as in the late 1920s, while productivity has been on the rise the incomes of the large majority of the population have seen little increase. What makes this a recipe for economic dislocation is that such a large proportion of overall income is in the hands of a very small percentage of the population. To keep the economy growing under such conditions, the very affluent and the rich need to spend and invest at a continuously high rate. In recent years the press has issued ample reports about the vast expenditures on new homes, cars, yachts, and art by corporate executives who have been the recipients of multi-million-dollar bonuses. There were only so many five-figure dinners that the members of this set could throw, however, or safaris on which they could embark. Along with lavish personal lives, the wealthy were needed as sources of investment. As it turned out, much of their capital, directly or indirectly, was channelled into investment in the speculative housing market.

———————

Those hoping that the financial crisis would not deeply damage the "real" economy received devastating news in early January 2009. U.S. retail chains reported that their holiday shopping sales had been dismal, among the worst in decades. So much for the so-called "Christmas miracle" that some had counted on. For many retailers in the United States, holiday-season sales account for between 25 per cent and 40 per cent of annual sales. In November and December 2008, retail sales dropped by 2.2 per cent compared with the previous year. According to the International Council of Shopping Centers, it was the largest decline since at least 1970.

Even Wal-Mart, widely regarded as recession-proof because of its relatively low prices, reported a weaker than anticipated holiday season, with a same-store sales increase of 1.7 per cent in December.

Many specialty retail stores were savaged during the holiday period. Sales in the specialty outlets of Neiman Marcus, including Neiman Marcus stores and Bergdorf Goodman, fell by 31.2 per cent in comparison with the previous year; sales at Saks dropped by 19.9 per cent. Other retailers experienced sharp year-to-year declines during the holidays. Abercrombie and Fitch was down 24 per cent; American Eagle Outfitters, 17 per cent; Gap, 14 per cent; and J.C. Penney, 7.3 per cent. Macy's, whose same-store sales dropped 4 per cent in December, announced that it would close eleven stores. It said they were "underperforming."

Making matters worse for surviving retailers was the impact of the bankruptcies of competing firms earlier in the year. Liquidation sales were held at bankrupt retail outlets of Linens 'n Things and Mervyns, among others. These sales cut into the business of those still afloat.[9]

The clearest signal that the financial crisis had leached into the wider economy came in January 2009, when U.S. government data revealed that employers shed 524,000 jobs in December. The total number of jobs lost in the United States in the last four months of 2008 was 1.9 million. For the year as a whole 2.6 million jobs disappeared. It was the largest job loss in a single year since 1945, when 2.75 million were shed in the final year of the Second World War as the United States was in transition to a peacetime economy.[10]

At 7.2 per cent, the U.S. unemployment rate was the highest since 1993. The official unemployment rate significantly understated the joblessness disaster. Millions of so-called "discouraged" workers, those who had given up looking for work, were not counted as being unemployed. In addition, more than eight million people were working part-time because they could not find full-time jobs. When those two cohorts are factored in, the proportion of the U.S. labour force that was effectively unemployed shot up to 13.5 per cent. By March 2009 the official U.S. unemployment rate had reached 8.5 per cent.[11]

While the Canadian job loss figures were proportionately not as bad as the U.S. numbers in December 2008, they were nonetheless alarming—revealing that Canada was swiftly following the United States into a severe recession. With the loss of 70,700 full-time jobs in December 2008, the country's unemployment rate rose to 6.6 per cent from 6.3 per cent in November. The creation of 36,200 part-time jobs softened the blow somewhat, although part-time work comes with lower pay, fewer benefits, and reduced job security.[12]

Although Alberta's unemployment rate, at 4.1 per cent, up 0.7 per cent from November, remained the lowest among the provinces, nearly 20,000 full-time jobs were lost there, the largest single provincial decline. Alberta's red-hot economy, centred on the oil sands, had slowed sharply in a period of only a few months. Keeping the unemployment numbers relatively low was the fact that thousands of contract workers left Alberta to return to their homes in other provinces when the heat came off the boom. As a consequence of falling oil prices, the massive expansion of oil sands projects that had been anticipated in early 2008 was scaled back appreciably. Many oil sands projects fell dormant. Investment in the oil sands for 2009 would go down by 20 per cent from 2008, to a total of $16 billion.[13]

Much more shocking news was revealed to Canadians on February 6, 2009. In January, 129,000 jobs were lost, the worst job loss ever recorded for a single month. Some 5 per cent of employment in the manufacturing sector was wiped out in that terrible month. With the loss of 71,000 jobs, Ontario was hardest hit, its unemployment rate soaring from 7.2 per cent to 8.0 per cent in January. Quebec and British Columbia also shed large numbers of jobs, with Quebec's unemployment rate rising to 7.7 per cent from 7.3 per cent, while British Columbia's rate climbed from 5.3 per cent to 6.2 per cent. The national unemployment rate climbed from 6.6 per cent to 7.2 per cent.

While the Harper government had been claiming that the economic crisis was significantly worse in the United States than in Canada, the results for January 2009 wiped away that illusion. In January the United States lost 598,000 jobs.[14] While this prompted President Barack Obama to urge Congress to pass his stimulus package rapidly in an attempt to halt the economy's downward spiral, proportionately the U.S. numbers were less serious than those in Canada. (By March 2009 the official Canadian unemployment rate had climbed to 8.0 per cent.)[15]

By the time Canadians received the news about the terrible job losses in January 2009, the minority Harper government had won a crucial reprieve in the House of Commons. The day after Finance Minister Flaherty unveiled his budget, the newly minted leader of the Liberals, Michael Ignatieff, declared that the Liberals would vote to support the bill. In return for the essential support of his party, without which the government would have fallen, Ignatieff asked only that the Conservatives accept an amendment to the budget pledging periodic updates in Parliament on the implementation of the government's economic plan. This concession, so slight as barely to be worth such a designation, was conceded by the Conservatives in a heartbeat.

When January's jobless figures came out a week and a half after the unveiling of the budget, Harper poured cold water on the idea that yet more stimulus could be needed to reignite the Canadian economy.

The Harper government's economic strategy had been based on transforming Canada into an "energy superpower." This plan was now in ruins, a twenty-first-century reminder of the risks of putting all of the country's economic eggs in the basket of shifting foreign demand for resources—a lesson painfully learned countless times over the past four hundred years.

The scale of job losses in the last months of 2008 and at the start of 2009 made it clear that the government's insistence that Canada was in a stronger position to endure the economic crisis was becoming less true with every passing day.

Adding to the bleak economic picture at the beginning of 2009 was the vast indebtedness of Americans, a factor of the greatest importance in driving this crisis from banks and the stock market to the wider economy. The eleven-trillion-dollar U.S. government debt was sustained by purchases of U.S. Treasury Bills and other government securities by China, Japan, and other countries. The net debt of Americans as a whole to the rest of the world stood at several trillion dollars. The personal indebtedness of Americans had soared from just over U.S.$600 billion thirty-five years earlier to about U.S.$10 trillion in 2009.

The year 2009 began with both hope and an enormous bailout package. Obama's inauguration as the forty-fourth president of the United States symbolized the continuing capacity of the United

States to return to its core values in a time of immense crisis. Following the barren years of the Bush presidency, the renewal of U.S. politics that brought Obama to the fore promised the possibility of a revival of the American socio-economic system, the kind of renewal that was successfully achieved during the presidency of Franklin D. Roosevelt between 1933 and 1945.

Obama's economic package promised stimulus to restart the engines of the U.S. economy. But it also added enormously to the indebtedness of Americans. The situation of the United States in 2009 was vastly different from that in the period of the Great Depression of the 1930s, when the United States was not only the world's leading industrial power but the leading creditor nation in the world. The United States had now become the world's leading debtor nation. With its existing economic structure and socio-economic arrangements, the United States was incapable of generating the capital needed to finance the Obama plan. As the incoming president predicted, the country would face trillion-dollar deficits for years to come—which would put enormous additional pressure on foreigners, especially the Chinese and the Japanese, to purchase even higher volumes of U.S. Treasury Bills.

In his book on the crash of 2008, financier George Soros wrote:

> This crisis is not confined to a particular firm or a particular segment of the financial system; it has brought the entire system to the brink of a breakdown, and it is being contained only with the greatest difficulty. This will have far-reaching consequences. It is not business as usual but the end of an era.[16]

With the onset of this economic crisis, then, one chapter in the economic history of the world is ending and a new one is beginning.

What we need now is to understand the forces that controlled the global system that has crashed and the forces that have the capacity to usher in the next global system. What is ending is the American-centred age of "globalization." For tens of millions of people, this is a perilous time as livelihoods are being destroyed. What comes next will depend on contending socio-economic forces in all parts of the world. It is, though, an exciting time because we are living in a period of open history, a time when the ideas of those who are normally locked out of meaningful decision-making can have a decisive impact on what happens in the years ahead.

Chapter Three

THE LIFE AND TIMES

OF SPECULATIVE BUBBLES

―――――――――

THE PROXIMATE CAUSE of the stock market crash of 2008 was the bursting of the speculative housing bubble. Why do such bubbles come into existence? Why have they roiled economies and societies not for a few years or even decades but for centuries?

A key is that without winners there would be no bubbles. While most people are ultimately victimized by a speculative bubble, not everyone loses. Indeed, some people become immensely wealthy as a consequence of a bubble. They keep their wealth long after the bubble has burst.

The causes of speculative bubbles are diverse. They include the perception of opportunities for wealth creation, the nature of government regulation, a sudden feverish rush to realize profits in a particular economic sector, and the psychology and mythologies of capitalist societies.

A speculative bubble develops when a number of forces converge and reinforce each other to produce a lethal or toxic result. It helps to start with the psychology, not because it is the most important cause of a bubble, but because it reveals how difficult it is for most people to understand a bubble at its zenith and to resist its feverish temptations. All bubbles are based on overgeneralizations about an area of activity in which real economic potential could exist.

Incredible as it may seem, one of the first speculative bubbles to hit the capitalist world came in the tulip industry of the Netherlands in the seventeenth century. Tulips became highly fashionable. New varieties were developed and a lucrative industry was established. (The Netherlands remains the cut-flower capital of the world today, exporting its products to many parts of the globe.) Financiers and wealthy citizens rushed to invest in tulips. The tulip bubble lasted from 1620 to 1637. At the peak of the craze, a rare and desirable tulip bulb could fetch a price as high as a house. When the bubble finally burst, the price of tulips crashed, and many people lost fortunes and were wiped out. We might all chuckle and say that we would never be taken in by such foolish speculation. Remember, though, that tulip-growing, then and now, is a viable industry, with profits to be made.

The most famous bubble in British history was the South Sea Bubble of the 1720s. The term "South Sea Bubble" is still a synonym for a dubious, speculative financial scheme.

In 1720 the House of Lords passed the South Sea Bill, establishing a monopoly in British trade with South America for the South Sea Company. The monopoly came in return for a loan of £7 million from the company to help finance the country's warmaking capacity. Throughout the eighteenth century the British government had to struggle mightily to finance the rising national debt that was the consequence of its frequent wars. The South Sea Company's loan to the British government underwrote the national debt, which then amounted to £30 million. In return the company received 5 per cent interest from the British state.

South Sea speculation took off as shares in the South Sea Company soared to ten times their face value. From the reasonable premise that there was a market in South America worth a great deal and the idea that financing the national debt could be profitable came all kinds of odd, related ventures. One enterprise proposed to purchase the Irish bogs. Another promised to manufacture square cannon balls. Yet another boasted of a highly profitable undertaking whose nature would not be revealed.

Fortunes were amassed, and then the bubble burst. People all over Britain lost money; many lost all of their money. Stocks crashed and investors who had known momentary riches were condemned to poverty. Among those ruined were ordinary Britons and members of the upper classes. Aristocrats lost fortunes, as did members of the clergy, including bishops. Two mistresses of King George I, the Countess of Darlington and the Duchess of Kendal, both of whom had been associated with the South Sea Company, faced the wrath of an angry populace. Riots broke out; suicides were frequent; and the Riot Act was read to restore calm.

A parliamentary inquiry into the affair led to the downfall of the chancellor of the Exchequer and the expulsion of several members of Parliament. Robert Walpole, generally regarded as Britain's first prime minister, had been an opponent of the South Sea Company from the start. He was appointed chancellor of the Exchequer, and he stepped in to clean up the financial mess. He divided up the national debt into three portions to be held by the Bank of England, the Treasury, and a newly created Sinking Fund. These measures are credited with restoring financial stability to the country.

For Americans, the classic speculative bubble blew up around the stampede to acquire real estate in Florida. In the mid-1920s, improved transportation and the rise of a class of well-heeled Americans who were anxious to avoid the rigours of winter in the Northeast or Midwest combined to make the development of winter getaways in Florida a booming industry. On Florida's east coast, Miami, Miami Beach, and Palm Beach became glittering names that drew tourists and investors. The warm waters and sunshine drew a similar rush to cities and towns on the Gulf of Mexico.

Again, the ingredients for the making of a speculative bubble were present. There was an economic opportunity, the scent of easy money to be made, and a weak regulatory framework that invited the quick-buck artists to do their work. The most famous of the artists, a man who gave his name to the filching of investors, was Charles Ponzi, a Bostonian who developed a subdivision that he described as being near Jacksonville—although, as it turned out, the land was sixty-five miles (over one hundred kilometres) west of the city.

Ponzi divided his land into compact lots, twenty-three to an acre, and told potential buyers that their property would be "not more than three fourths of a mile from the prosperous and fast-growing city of Nettie." The problem was that this so-called "city" did not exist.

By autumn 1925 the price of lots in Florida had shot up. Waterfront lots within forty miles of Miami sold for between U.S.$15,000 and $25,000 and "inside" lots fetched from $8,000 to $20,000. In 1926 things began to turn badly for those who had plunged into the Florida real estate boom. Fewer new buyers were coming forward, and a speculative boom such as this depended on a continuing supply of new buyers. That autumn two hurricanes hit the peninsula, one of them killing four hundred people.

Even though the bubble was deflating, cheerleaders continued to insist on the money to be made in Florida real estate. Writing in the *Wall Street Journal* on October 8, 1926, a representative of Seaboard Air Line insisted that despite the presence of thousands of people needing aid in the aftermath of the hurricane, "the same Florida is still there with its magnificent resources, its wonderful climate, and its geographical position. It is the Riviera of America."[1]

But by then the bubble had burst. The demise of the Florida land rush was reflected in Miami in the value of bank clearings, which plunged from just over U.S.$1 billion in 1925 to $143 million in 1928.[2] In the wake of the collapse many speculators lost their shirts, although their numbers were small in comparison to the great bloodletting that came as a consequence of the stock market crash of 1929. The bad feelings about the Florida land bubble are sustained by the popular notion that if someone is dumb enough, you should sell him some swampland in Florida. Today, in the wake of the sub-prime mortgage meltdown, parts of Florida are again acquiring a dubious reputation. For instance, Cape Coral just outside Fort Myers has been described "as the foreclosure capital of Florida."

———————————

A more recent speculative bubble developed around dot.com stocks in the late 1990s, only to be deflated with the subsequent dot.com crash in the spring of 2000. A classic of the genre, the tech craze

rested on the solid (if virtual) foundation of a revolutionary technology that was genuinely transforming communications, culture,
and the conduct of business. Around the rise of this novel sector
and the new companies that drove it, a mythology developed that
played a key role in suckering investors into the market.

The notion of the "new economy" rose alongside the rise of
dot.com stocks. The proponents of the new economy proclaimed
that communications technology had become the new engine
of the economic system and that the rise of this sector had rele-
gated the economic cycle, with its ups and downs, booms and busts,
to the past. As the prices of dot.com stocks soared, the champions
of these investments argued that it did not much matter whether
the dot.com companies made profits or paid dividends. According
to these cheerleaders, the key to success was a torrid rate of expansion. Expanding the company's customer base and strengthening
the search engine of the company were what mattered, not the
profits of the venture.

During the peak of the frenzy, dot.com companies appeared on
the market with little capitalization and no track record and managed to raise huge amounts of capital with their Initial Public
Offering (IPO). At Super Bowl XXXIV, in January 2000, seventeen
dot.com companies paid over U.S.$2 million each for a thirty-
second television commercial. The dot.com commercials were so
hot that broadcasters talked more about them than about the poor
sods on the field.

The idea—insisted the proponents of the new economy, of
which the dot.com companies were the champions—that there
ought to be a reasonable price to earnings ratio for a stock was so
"yesterday." The price to earnings ratio (P/E) tells an investor how
much the market is willing to pay to acquire a company's earnings.

A stock with a low P/E ratio is often a stock seen as highly risky. In such a case the market is not willing to pay a high price to obtain the company's earnings. On the other hand, a stock with a high P/E ration is seen as a stock that is very desirable. It is one that investors believe is likely to soar in value. In such a case, investors may be prepared to accept a relatively low return for what they think will be a stock that will rise in price. Here the investor is interested in how much can be made on the value of the stock rather than on the earnings it generates. Stocks with a high P/E ratio are often flashing warning signs of the presence of a speculative bubble, as turned out to be the case with dot.com stocks.

A frenzied market grew up around the dot.coms. They were pedalled as being so desirable that even though many never earned a profit they were bound to keep on going up in value. Plenty of investment advisors and media business analysts poured kerosene on the fire, telling investors that the opportunity was too good to miss.

On paper at least, dot.com companies, run by people who could scarcely afford a bicycle a few months earlier, were suddenly valued at tens of millions of dollars. It was the Florida land rush all over again, although this time it was a virtual land rush. By the time the dot.com craze was in full swing, Microsoft had already become a global giant; its founder, Bill Gates, was the richest man in the world. Some of the newcomers became and remain household names: Amazon.com, Yahoo!, and Google among them. A long list of other companies achieved fifteen minutes of fame: they raised millions of dollars and perished when the dot.com bubble burst. Members of this passing parade included 360HipHop, billed as "the ultimate hip-hop destination on the web"; Broadband Sports, a sports-centred set of sites; DigiScents, an operation that attempted to transmit smells to its subscribers; Flooz.com, which tried to set itself up as an online currency, with Whoopi Goldberg as its spokesperson; Kibu.com, an online site for teenage girls; and Yadayada.com, an Internet browser service based in New York. Among other things, Yadayada provided rankings of public bathrooms, according to cleanliness and accessibility, in Manhattan. In 2001 the company went bust and laid off its workers. Meanwhile the CEO of this failed enterprise was rumoured to have taken off to Canada.

The NASDAQ, the tech-heavy New York stock exchange, soared in the late 1990s, its composite index cruising past 5,000 points in early 2000. On March 10 of that year the NASDAQ composite index peaked at 5,048.62. Then came the crash. Over the weekend of March 11 and 12, investors dumped the stocks of Cisco, IBM, and Dell (major NASDAQ listings) in massive pre-sell orders, which were processed on the morning of Monday, March 13. The NASDAQ composite index fell four percentage points at the opening of trading. This sell-off generated a panic as investors rushed to the exits. By Wednesday the NASDAQ had dropped 9 per cent in under a week. On December 31, 2000, the NASDAQ composite closed out the disastrous year at 2,470.52. But that was not the end of the doldrums for the once mighty high-tech exchange. On September 21, 2001, the NASDAQ plumbed a new low at 1,423.19, and it went still lower on October 4, 2002, to 1,139.90. After that the NASDAQ did rise from its deepest lows, but in subsequent years it did not come close to reaching the levels of the bubble days. On December 7, 2007, the composite index reached 2,706.16. From there, it slid somewhat and in the autumn of 2008, along with other stock markets, the NASDAQ headed relentlessly lower. On January 23, 2009, the composite index closed at 1,477.29.[3]

In addition to the many speculators who were ruined, the dot.com bubble and its subsequent bust wiped out ordinary investors who thought they were riding the wave of the future. The dream of the new economy was a casualty. In 2000, as the virtual economy dove, petroleum, a pillar of the old economy, soared in price. As it turned out, the economy had not changed as much as the prophets of the dot.com stocks had claimed.

As has been the case over the centuries, the drive towards new speculative bubbles remains a powerful tendency in capitalist economies. The appetite of the greedy to discover ways of turning a reasonable economic objective into the source of unfathomable wealth is enormously powerful, particularly in an economy in which the incomes of most people are not rising. Speculative bubbles are much like the growth of tumours: relentless and ultimately toxic, even lethal.

The bursting of the dot.com bubble had one specific consequence that was to be extremely significant for the future. Many investors who fled from high-tech as the NASDAQ sank were looking for another way of getting rich quick. A large number of them thought they had found it in the realm of housing, which would only prove to be the next bubble.

Chapter Four

THE HOUSING BUBBLE

AFTER THE RUPTURE of the dot.com bubble, housing was the logical place to go for many investors. Like the speculative bubbles that preceded it, the housing bubble blew up in a perfect storm of converging forces.

This speculative craze also began with a concept that everyone recognized as highly desirable: the ownership of a home. Much of the population of the United States, as well as of other countries, including Canada and the United Kingdom, was convinced that the ownership of a home was a key, if not the essential key, to the acquisition of substantially greater personal assets. Home ownership has long been understood as an essential part of the "American dream," and the sentiment is similar in other advanced countries as well.

When Margaret Thatcher's Conservative Party came to power in the United Kingdom in 1979, a key goal of her government was to push the number of homeowners up and the number of trade union members down so that the first group would come to exceed the second. In the early 1980s that objective was realized when Britain's ten million homeowners, many of them living in dwellings that were formerly publicly owned council flats, surpassed the membership of British unions. Thatcher and her ministers believed that a nation of homeowners would naturally adopt conservative values and shed a labourite outlook. The administration of U.S. president George W. Bush was equally wedded to the idea that promoting home ownership would win over Americans to conservatism and the Republican Party.

Beginning in 2005, when I became convinced that a real estate speculative bubble had developed and that this would lead inexorably to a real estate crash, I often encountered people who refused to believe that house prices would ever fall. When I predicted the coming collapse of housing prices in conversations with acquaintances and friends, I was met with stony disbelief and, in some cases, with annoyance, as though I were calling into question a cherished conviction that ought not to be challenged. Even when my broad proposition that house prices were about to fall was not challenged, people often made what we can call the "special case" argument. This line of reasoning is a favourite among those who are determined to cling to the siren message of a speculative frenzy even when it is coming under persistent challenge.

Housing speculation is particularly susceptible to the special case argument. All houses are not created equal, nor are all neighbourhoods. It is not easy to convince someone that a foreclosure crisis in Cleveland could somehow be connected to the price of a house in Vancouver's Kitsilano, in Manhattan, in London's West End, or in the Georgian row houses of Bath, England. In conversations, when I insisted that Vancouver, despite the Olympics, and London, despite the presence of highly affluent expatriate lawyers and financiers, would face declines in the value of houses, my opinions were regarded as rampant foolishness.

The psychology of the housing bubble was particularly perni-
cious because it fed on half-truths and on the dreams of millions of
people. For those who grew up in a family that owned a house, the
idea of home ownership as a wonderful way of saving money and
accumulating wealth is deeply entrenched. In Toronto my parents
purchased a house in 1946 for $8,800. In the summer of 2008 that
house would have fetched half a million dollars. That broad fact
says something, but it hides much. Sixty-two years is a long time, so
most of the nominal difference between the price at which they
bought the house in 1946 and the potential price of the house in
2008 was a consequence of inflation. Still, the real (accounting for
inflation) increase is substantial. The real value of the house in 2008
was about ten times its worth in 1946. A moderately good stock
would have done as well. What the increase in the real price hides is
that the house shot up in value during a number of specific periods,
but the price remained flat for much longer periods and actually
declined dramatically during others. For instance, in the year or
two after 1990, when real estate prices declined dramatically all over
the world as a consequence of the bursting of the Japanese real
estate speculative bubble, the real price of the house dropped by
about a third.

Despite these elementary realities, the idea that buying a house
will benefit you is so strongly entrenched that even after house
prices began to fall sharply in many parts of the world in autumn
2008, and despite the constant media coverage of the global economic meltdown, I continue to encounter people who think that
they would do well if they purchased a house. After all, they reason,
the price has already fallen. Better to get in on the ground floor
before prices shoot up again. What they fail to grasp is that the
price has only begun to fall and it is likely to fall still further. Any

increase in the price of the house is probably years away. In the meantime, such a prospective purchaser would do better to put his or her money under a mattress.

The next argument you encounter is that buying a house can be a form of "forced saving" in a family that requires the discipline of monthly mortgage payments to avoid squandering any money they have left after paying for the necessities of life. My response is that a savings program that begins with a substantial decline of real assets and a vastly increased debt burden is rather hare-brained.

The Bush administration was adept at playing on the enormous public sentiment in favour of home ownership in promoting its own agenda on the issue. To overcome the fundamental problem that house prices were shooting upwards while most personal incomes remained stagnant, the Bush administration tried to find ways of allowing people to purchase homes despite the high risk of new homeowners not being able to cope with the mortgages they were taking on. What the president and his officials wanted was mortgages with no down payments. In his quest to make home-buying easier, Bush called on mortgage brokers and financial institutions to do their part. Speaking on the subject of home ownership, the president declared, "Corporate America has a responsibility to work to make America a compassionate place."[1]

Financiers, seeing a vast opportunity to get rich out of this sector, came up with mortgage schemes designed precisely to ensnare lenders in arrangements whose implications were not fully understood. Lending institutions offered mortgages with so-called teaser rates, so that the purchasers paid a very low rate to start—a rate that later grew sharply higher. They also unveiled interest-only loans, which were designed so that the buyer paid only interest and never paid down the principal on the loan. For the buyer, this was a purely speculative venture. Unless the house went up in value, the buyer was stuck paying what amounted to rent, with no end in sight. And, of course, if the house should fall in value, the purchaser was locked into endless payments on a depreciating asset, a virtual invitation to default.

———————

During the 2004 election campaign, mortgage bankers and brokers donated nearly U.S.$850,000 to the Bush re-election campaign, more than three times the amount they contributed for the campaign in 2000. In 2004 Roland Arnall, the founder of Ameriquest, the country's largest lender of sub-prime mortgages, was among the Republican Party's top ten donors. In July 2005 Ameriquest had to allocate U.S.$325 million to settle allegations in thirty states that it had saddled borrowers with hidden fees and sharply rising payments after initial bargain payments.[2] Instead of paying heed to this warning sign that sub-prime mortgages were threatening the country with a foreclosure crisis, the Bush administration spent its time making sure that Arnall, the president's nominee as the U.S. ambassador to the Netherlands, received Senate confirmation.

Plenty of critics were around to warn of the consequences to come from these lending practices. In December 2005 Brian Montgomery, the commissioner of the Federal Housing Administration, in a memo that he drew to the attention of the White House, pointed to the risks of the lending practices of companies such as Ameriquest. Montgomery's agency was responsible for insuring home loans for low-income buyers.

More than two years earlier, Armando Falcon Jr., the head of the Office of Federal Housing Enterprise Oversight, issued a blistering warning about where things were heading. His agency was a watchdog that oversaw Fannie Mae and Freddie Mac, two giant companies created by the U.S. Congress in the 1930s. Freddie and Fannie, whose job was to buy trillions of dollars' worth of mortgages, could hold the mortgages or sell them off as guaranteed securities to investors. Falcon's February 2003 report, for which the Bush administration summarily fired him, warned that the two giants could end up defaulting on debt, which he predicted would set off "contagious illiquidity in the market"—in other words, the kind of financial crisis that did eventually occur. Falcon also sounded the alarm about the enormous use that Freddie and Fannie made of derivatives, financial instruments that enticed investors to think they could make a killing on commodities, currencies, and securities.

Derivatives can yield immense profits for those who purchase them, and they are used by investors to hedge their bets on how things will turn out in the future. These instruments of the futures markets allow investors to bet on how the orange crop in Florida will turn out, whether the euro will go up or down in value against some other currency, or what the price of oil will be in six months. An investor can put up a very small amount of capital and make a very large bet. This is a twenty-first-century version of buying on margin, a strategy that played a big role in the stock market crash of 1929.

A derivative that has now become dangerously prevalent is the purchase by investors of "shorts" on investments that they want to see rise in value. When you purchase a "short," you are betting that a particular investment will be lower in value by some specified date in the future. Investors use this technique as a form of insurance in case the investments that are central to their ambitions, the ones they hope will soar upwards, actually fall.

The problem is that the insurance provided in this way turned out to be a fool's paradise.

In 2007 the Bush administration received another warning from a young White House economic analyst who became concerned about what was happening to one crucial housing market statistic: the rent-to-own ratio. Under normal conditions, when housing prices rise, so do rents. Jason Thomas, the analyst, produced charts for top administration officials that revealed that the cost of owning a house was soaring upwards far faster than was the cost of renting a similar property.3 This was a flashing warning, and a rather obvious one, that a speculative housing bubble existed—that the high housing prices would prove unsustainable, and that a crisis was in the offing.

Not only was the Bush administration unwilling to enhance the ability of regulators to take action to head off the risk of a housing meltdown—its inclination was to do quite the opposite—but U.S. tax policy had also long skewed investments towards the housing market. For decades, U.S. home buyers have been entitled to deduct mortgage interest payments from their taxable incomes. This policy, long seen as a form of middle-class entitlement, had dramatically contributed to the growth of suburbs and edge cities at the expense of urban downtowns and public transit. It channelled capital into housing purchases and cut back the tax revenues that governments had for education, urban renewal, and other spending areas. In addition to this long-existing measure, a tax measure proposed by the Clinton administration and approved by Congress in 1997 further funnelled capital into housing. The measure sheltered most homeowners from having to pay capital gains taxes on the increase in the value of their homes when they sold them. For a married couple, the first U.S.$500,000 in capital gains from a sale of a house, provided they had lived in it for two of the previous five years, were exempt (for singles, the exemption covered the first U.S.$250,000 in capital gains).⁴ The measure discriminated in favour of investments in the purchase of houses, as compared with the purchase of stocks or bonds, where capital gains were taxable at rates of up to 20 per cent.

This tax measure helped promote the idea that for Americans the purchase of a home was much more than the acquisition of a place to live. It was an investment, a money-making activity. An economist at the Federal Reserve Board who studied the impact of this tax measure concluded that the number of houses sold over the past decade was nearly 17 per cent higher than it would have been without the capital gains exemption.⁵

The rising price of housing had a pronounced effect on the behaviour of millions of people not just in the United States, but in many other countries, including the United Kingdom and Canada. Those with homes for which mortgages had been paid off borrowed money on the asset value of those homes to use for other purposes. In Britain a favourite use for borrowed money was to purchase property on the continent, particularly in France. In many regions of France, among them Provence, the Côte d'Azur, and the Dordogne, British buyers in search of blue skies and warmer winters purchased "*maisons secondaires*," in many cases profoundly altering the character of the affected communities. Prices of homes and property were driven up so that local inhabitants often found it impossible to purchase property in towns and rural areas that their families had lived in for generations.

In Canada the "wealth effect" experienced by those who owned homes for which value was soaring spurred owners to make major renovations to the homes and to purchase lakefront property. In Ontario the price of cottages shot up in fashionable Muskoka and Haliburton. The concept of the cottage was transformed from that of a rustic dwelling for summer enjoyment to a country mansion with all the conveniences. Especially on the major lakes, cottage properties were selling for many millions of dollars. Driving the rush to buy property in cottage country were not only lifestyle aspirations but the speculative lure of rising prices.

Once the housing bubble burst, all of the logic worked in reverse. As property values dropped, mortgages became a burden, an albatross for millions of people. Instead of spurring additional spending and investing as the house market had when prices were rising, the housing market had the effect of depressing spending and reducing investments. It became a dead weight that dragged the economy down.

Chapter Five

THE PERILS OF DEFLATION

THE BURSTING of the housing bubble, the failure of financial institutions, and the crash of stock markets around the globe struck investors, the rich, and the well-to-do with the force of a tsunami. The consequence was a sharp decline in the high-end spending of those who had accumulated money and now suddenly had less. As in the 1929 crash, the sharp reduction in spending and investing by the wealthy and near-wealthy played a signal role in spreading the crisis from financial markets to the "real" economy.

Layoffs in the retail sector, bankruptcies, and bankruptcy sales pushed the economy down the dismal road of sharply rising unemployment and deflation. While most of us have experienced inflation and the falling value of the dollars we hold, very few alive today have suffered deflation, a far more deadly economic affliction. On the surface, deflation, a condition that arises when prices fall, has its attractions. Few motorists in Canada complained about the substantial drop in the price of gasoline after the summer of 2008, and few homeowners complained about the 30 per cent decline in the price of fuel to heat their houses. The problem with deflation is that it is symptomatic of a severe economic downturn that can last not for a few months but for years, crossing the line from recession to depression. Throughout the industrialized world, economic policy-makers are grappling with the onset of deflation. Its devastation can be seen, among other places, in the crisis of the automobile industry.

When deflation strikes an economy, the prospects for economic growth are so negative that companies not only lay off large num-bers of employees but also put on hold capital investment projects that are a key to future growth and the hiring of additional workers. For instance, the catastrophic sales declines in late 2008 at the major automobile companies signalled the need for a drastic reorgani-zation of the industry. In December 2008, Chrysler's sales of auto-mobiles in the United States plunged 50 per cent in comparison to the previous December. This left analysts concluding that Chrysler could not long survive as a separate auto producer. Many pre-dicted that what remained of Chrysler would have to be merged with General Motors, which would also have to be dramatically downsized. While the price bargains subsequently offered by the two ailing automakers had never been better, at the end of the restructuring the U.S. auto industry would employ tens of thou-sands fewer workers than it did at the start of 2008. Cities, towns, and entire states would be dramatically set back by the lurch of the economy into deflation.

The evidence that deflation has struck the global economy is widely visible. It is there to be seen in the crash in the U.S. housing market, in the plunge in housing prices in Britain, and in the slower but advancing drop in housing prices in Canada. The plunge in the price of petroleum is another sign, as is the 66 per cent decline in the price of copper, the 73 per cent decline in lead and nickel prices, the 66 per cent decline in the price of platinum, and the 64 per cent drop in the price of wheat. Then too, as the prices of commodities went into free fall, those who sell goods and services to consumers rushed to slash their prices. Even the prices of the most popular automobiles became lower than they were a few years earlier. A 2009 Toyota Camry sold for $2,000 less than a 2001 Camry did when it was new. Auto-dealers in the United States began to sell cars at such reduced prices that they did not fully cover the cost of manufacturing the vehicles. Tour operators dropped prices for trips abroad, for cruises on the seas and oceans, and for flights.

Deflation negates the motivation for business to make capital investments. The reason is quite simple. As consumer purchases decline, the prospect for increased sales diminishes. Rather than making investments—which involves hiring more workers, either by the company itself or through its suppliers, to expand plant capacity, to purchase new machinery, or to design new products— the company reduces production and lays off some of its existing employees. The company sells off its inventory, reducing prices to capture as large a share of the shrinking market for itself as it can. The consequence of this behaviour is that the ranks of the unemployed are expanded. Consumer purchasing power is further reduced, which lowers demand further, driving the system through successive rounds of layoffs and deepening deflation.

———————

Evidence that deflation was the order of the day accumulated in a number of countries during the winter and spring of 2009. In May 2009 the Office for National Statistics in the United Kingdom reported that inflation, as measured by the Retail Prices Index, was -1.2 per cent in April. In other words, Britain was experiencing deflation, as prices fell, according to the reporting body, more steeply than at any time since 1948. The -1.2 per cent figure for April was steeper than the figure for the previous month, which was -0.4 per cent. Brendan Barber, the general secretary of Britain's Trades Union Congress, warned that "entrenched deflation would be a real threat to economic recovery." Jonathan Loynes of Capital Economics, a U.K. research consultancy, commented, "The numbers should be a reminder to markets and policymakers that excessively low inflation, and even deflation, remains a bigger risk over the next year or two, than a sharp upturn in inflation."[1]

In May 2009 Statistics Canada reported that the annual rate of inflation, as measured in its consumer price index (cpi), fell more than expected in April, to 0.4 per cent from 1.2 per cent in March. This was the lowest level for the cpi in fourteen years.[2] Alberta, whose economy had led the nation during the lead-up to the crash, posted the biggest provincial decline in consumer prices, with an inflation rate of -0.7 per cent. Sharply falling energy prices were responsible for Alberta's descent into deflation.[3] Reporting that same month to a parliamentary committee on the state of the nation's economy, Bank of Canada governor Mark Carney anticipated that "total inflation will temporarily fall below zero in 2009." The bank governor reported that Canada would experience a deeper recession than the Bank of Canada had forecast in its mildly rosy report issued in January 2009.[4] In late July 2009 the Bank of Canada again altered its forecast, issuing a more optimistic report on the trajectory of the Canadian economy. Now, in contrast to its spring forecast, the Bank was predicting that the economy would expand by an annualized rate of 1.3 per cent during the third quarter of 2009. While foreseeing the technical end of the recession, which had endured for nine months, Carney cautioned that it would take more than a year to replace the wealth destroyed by the financial crisis. This time—after being previously stung at the beginning of 2009 after making the too-rosy economic forecast—Carney was careful to warn that the recovery both at home and globally still faced risks and that the resumption of growth would be slower than was usually the case following a recession. Along with his prediction of an anemic recovery, Carney said he did not expect a return to a pre-recessionary rate of inflation.[5]

The U.S. economy was also following the deflationary trend experienced in other countries. During 2008 the U.S. inflation rate averaged 3.85 per cent. Over the course of the year the rate peaked at 5.6 per cent in July, coincident with very high gasoline prices, and then declined to .09 per cent in December, by which time the economic crisis was in full swing. In March and April 2009 the United States entered the realm of deflation with inflation rates of -0.38 per cent and -0.74 per cent respectively.[6]

In September 2008, just as the stock market crash was getting underway, *New York Times* columnist Paul Krugman warned that the United States risked being dragged down by what he depicted as "debt deflation," the disease that had plagued Japan following the bursting of its property price bubble at the end of the 1980s. Krugman provided a good description of "debt deflation":

As the economist Irving Fisher observed way back in 1933, when highly indebted individuals and businesses get into financial trouble, they usually sell assets and use the proceeds to pay down their debt. What Fisher pointed out, however, was that such selloffs are self-defeating when everyone does it: if everyone tries to sell assets at the same time, the resulting plunge in market prices undermines debtors' financial positions faster than debt can be paid off. So deflation in asset prices can turn into a vicious circle. And one consequence of what he called a "stampede to liquidate" is a severe economic slump.[7]

The deflationary downward spiral during the Great Depression was not self-correcting, as it turned out. Orthodox neo-classical economists and right-wing politicians are wedded to the idea that markets, when left alone by governments, will work out these problems on their own. They believe that if the price of labour (wages and salaries) is allowed to fall, along with consumer prices, a point will be reached at which companies will once again find it profitable to make investments and increase production. This way, they insist, the downward spiral, if allowed to work itself out, will reverse, to be followed by an upward virtuous economic cycle.

From that point of view the culprits standing in the way of economic renewal are trade unions that keep the price of labour artificially high, and governments that stand in the way of allowing wages and salaries to fall by paying out unemployment insurance and social assistance to the unemployed. Right-wing orthodoxy insists that the price of labour should be allowed to fall to the point at which it becomes profitable to rehire workers.

In late 2008 in the United States and Canada, right-wingers were quick to make unionized auto workers the poster boys for what was wrong with the auto industry. The wages of auto workers had to drop dramatically, they insisted, for the auto companies to return to viability. Using the same logic, right-wing thinkers and

politicians, in principle, are opposed to the implementation of minimum wages, and are utterly against raising them. Minimum wages,
they say, are uneconomic. Minimum wages make the price of
labour "sticky" to the downside—hard to push down. They stand in
the way of the market sorting things out so that the drive to prosperity can be resumed.

That is not to say that right-wingers and their intellectual man-
darins, who populate the business schools of the United States and
Canada, are opposed to all public policy measures being undertaken to cope with a severe economic downturn. They favour three
types of actions by governments under such circumstances. First,
they approve of central banks lowering interest rates to make it less
costly for businesses to borrow and invest capital and for individuals to purchase automobiles, other durable goods, or houses.
Second, they applaud governments that make deep tax cuts, on the
assumption that this will put more money in the pockets of people
and in the coffers of business, which will allow consumer spending
to rebound along with new capital investments. Third, they favour
sharply reducing government spending, as a corollary to the tax
cuts. This, they say, will keep deficit spending by governments to a
minimum, with the additional attraction of permanently reducing
the role of government in favour of the market, which is an over-
riding objective of theirs.

The problem with this right-wing agenda, and its individual
elements, is that it does not work. Its measures were tried for years
during the Great Depression. The consequence of this dreary
experiment was utter failure. The dirty little secret of neo-classical
economics is that left to its own devices a market economy can
achieve a point of equilibrium between supply and demand that
leaves millions of people, a high proportion of the workforce,

without employment. An equilibrium can exist that leaves economic output far below full capacity.

This is the ground on which the great disputes between the Keynesians and the monetarists were fought out.

John Maynard Keynes made the case that neo-classical economics had not solved the problem of the possibility of an economic equilibrium being achieved without full employment or full utilization of economic capacity, or anything close to it, being realized. He insisted that governments had to play an indispensable role in ensuring that sufficient demand existed to allow the economy to function at, or near, full capacity. In addition to the stimulus provided by monetary policy, through interest rate cuts, there had to be the stimulus directly provided by direct government spending, as well as through tax cuts, not to the wealthy but to the mass of the population.

As deflation sucks the economy downward, people discover the consequences for themselves at different times. Construction and automobile workers learn the lesson very early on in the process. A little later, retail workers find out what it means. Then come the employees of restaurants, hotels, airlines, and a host of other service providers. Cities, towns, and whole regions feel the pain at different times depending on the nature of their economies. Cities whose livelihoods are closely tied to the auto industry find themselves with depression-level consequences while other cities are still feeling the milder symptoms of recession. But the direction is inexorably downward for the whole economy, and the descent does not stop and reverse according to some rule of the marketplace. Only governments can reverse the process, with an effort and with the application of resources that can be likened to the mobilization to fight a war.

Those who oversee the contemporary economy—central bankers and top government policy-makers—are well aware of the great deflation of the 1930s. Some of the policies of the Federal Reserve Board in the United States and of the U.S. federal government after the autumn of 2008, in the last days of the Bush administration and the first days of the Obama administration, were aimed at halting the descent into deflation. During autumn 2008, as conditions worsened and the flow of credit dried up in the United States, the Bush administration took steps through its acquisition of Fannie Mae and Freddie Mac and through the pumping of funds from the Troubled Assets Relief Program (TARP) into financial institutions to relieve them of the burdens of toxic sub-prime mortgages. In mid-October the Bush administration revised the TARP operations so that the Treasury could purchase preferred, non-voting stock in the largest U.S. banks. With new regulations in place after taking office, the Obama administration continued to pump TARP funds into financial institutions. On March 23, 2009, Treasury Secretary Timothy Geithner announced the creation of a Public-Private Investment Program (P-PIP) to purchase the toxic assets of the banks. Stock markets rallied after hearing news of the program.

The enormous use of public funds to relaunch financial institutions and get credit flowing to businesses and consumers was intended to counter the shock of deflation. As the Federal Reserve and the U.S. government fought their war against deflation they were taking a gigantic risk—that further down the road the policies they were pursuing could generate massive inflation. It was the very opposite of the problem they were seeking to address.

In the U.S. case, the reason that the risk of inflation is high over the longer term is that the country is so massively indebted in different ways to the rest of the world. The enormous expansion of the money supply being undertaken by the Fed and the U.S. Treasury can have the effect of monetizing the U.S. government debt, in effect by watering down the value of the currency. The consequence of this will be to put downward pressure on the value of the U.S. dollar against other currencies. Both the monetization of the debt and the fall in the dollar can unleash inflation—potentially inflation that, once begun, will be self-generating.

Chapter Six

INCOME AND WEALTH

INEQUALITY: AN UNDERLYING

CAUSE OF THE CRASH

———————

THE LAST THIRTY YEARS have been the golden age of inequality. While that inequality was the incubator for multitudes of new billionaires, it was, as well, a principal cause of the crash. In large part the meltdown of the financial sector flowed from the labour-market model that was the very heart of neo-liberalism. The financial meltdown flowed directly from the reckless decisions of financial managers to mine the economy for enhanced profits through the promotion of various kinds of debt and the promotion of a variety of financial products whose common aim was to heighten the leverage of investors.

In sharp contrast to the period from 1950 to 1970, when the real incomes of the families of wage- and salary-earning Canadians, adjusted for inflation, doubled,[1] during the last several decades real incomes in North America have remained essentially flat for most wage and salary earners.

In the period 1980 to 2006, what happened to the incomes of younger U.S. full-time, full-year wage and salary earners aged twenty-five to thirty-four is telling. This cohort is extraordinarily important because it is made up of people already solidly in the workforce. They are people for whom a pattern has been set and whose life journeys will be crucial in coming decades. In constant 2006 dollars, the median annual income of this crucial cohort in 1980 was U.S.$36,700; in 2006, it was $35,000. The men in this cohort had median wage and salary figures of U.S.$43,700 for 1980 and $37,000 for 2006. The similar figures for women were U.S.$29,400 and $31,800; for whites of both genders, U.S.$38,200 and $37,400; for blacks of both genders, U.S.$29,400 and $30,000; and for Hispanics of both genders, U.S.$33,000 and $28,000.[2]

The median incomes for working-age U.S. households over the period from 2001 to 2007—the years in the lead-up to the crash— are also revealing. Household incomes are crucially important to economic well-being, including as they do the incomes of single-income households and the larger number of households that have more than one earner. In constant 2007 dollars, the median income of working-age U.S. households was U.S.$58,721 in 2001; in 2007, it was $56,545.[3]

In Canada the median wages and salaries of Canadian workers, adjusted for inflation, have not grown for the past three decades. A study published by the Canadian Centre for Policy Alternatives resolves the different ways in which Statistics Canada has categorized the data to show that average real wages for Canadian workers have not increased since the end of the 1970s. In constant 2005 Canadian dollars, the average weekly wage was just under $800 in the early 1980s, and it remained at that level in 2005, with those working overtime earning more than those who did not. While minor fluctuations occurred over the decades, what is remarkable is how little things changed. Rising levels of productivity in the economy were not passed on to the average worker in the form of higher wages. The study concluded: "Astoundingly . . . real wages have been stagnant for 30 years running."[4]

During an epoch in which the top 1 per cent of income earners were squeezing ever more out of the economy for themselves, employers and governments, with the full support of neo-liberal economists and social scientists, were implementing a labour-market model that marginalized an ever larger proportion of the workforce. Particularly in the Anglo-American world and in countries that adopted the Anglo-American model, the dominant idea was to establish an ever more "flexible" labour market. The word "flexible," chosen to seem modern and progressive, meant that the labour force would be segmented: its inner core would be made up of wage and salary earners with full-time employment, benefits, and a degree of job security; around this core an ever greater secondary labour force would be made up of part-time or contractual employees. The rate of pay of this secondary workforce would be lower, and those people would have few benefits, be without pensions, and have little or no job security. Over the past quarter-century the rise of this secondary or precarious labour force has transformed the economies of the advanced countries.

For the most part, the precarious labour force has been made up of women, immigrants, people of colour, migrants to cities from rural areas and small towns, and those with limited education. The workers in the precarious labour force cost employers, whether they are in the private or public sectors, much less than do their employees in the inner or permanent labour force. Savings accrue in a number of ways. The hourly or weekly rates of pay of precarious workers are lower. Reduced benefits and the absence of pensions result in enormous savings. Of great importance, the members of the precarious work force can be hired or laid off at the pleasure of the employer or, to use the in-word, in the most *flexible* possible way. As the demand for goods and services rises in particular sectors, people can be hired, without long-term commitments being made to them, so that when demand declines, these people can be shown the door with little difficulty.

The rise of the precarious or secondary labour force also puts immense pressure on the permanent labour force, by threatening it with a less costly alternative. The permanent labour force is highly expensive for employers. Wages and salaries are much higher than in the precarious zone; benefits are substantial and costly, and so too are pensions. In addition, depending on labour laws in particular jurisdictions, as well as union contracts, dismissing an employee can be an expensive affair, often involving costly severance payouts. Another highly significant factor is that the permanent labour force is much more often unionized than is the precarious force.

Unions manage to increase the wages, salaries, benefits, and job security of their members. The proponents of a flexible labour market believe that these effects of trade unionism are undesirable. Business school students are taught that trade unionism is old-fashioned. While it once played a useful role in winning higher wages and better working conditions for employees in the days of the rough and ready capitalism of the past, capitalism has been modernized and humanized and no longer needs unions, the story goes. Instead, students learn, unions are barriers that stand in the way of efficiency, increased productivity, and the smooth evolution of the market economy towards providing ever more highly sought goods and services.

Neo-liberal economists contend that too much job security holds an economy back. Job security can block a company's move into cutting-edge sectors of the future, tempting the enterprise to remain in mature sectors that may already be in decline. Over the long term such a company is bound to lose out to more innovative companies that do not have to operate according these rules. In addition, job security, these analysts contend, forces enterprises to keep mediocre and aging employees on their payrolls, when they would do better if they could rid themselves of such workers and hire younger, better educated, more highly motivated people.

There is no doubt, as well, that competition and negative feelings between those in the permanent labour force and those in the marginalized workforce act to the benefit of both private- and public-sector employers. Part-time workers who are not unionized and who have little job security are often resentful of workers with full-time jobs who have substantial job security and the protection of union contracts. In neo-liberal societies the media regularly depict the elected officials of trade unions as "union bosses," suggesting that their members work for the union rather than the reverse. In the public service, which is now relatively highly unionized, especially in Canada, employees are routinely described as lazy and inefficient, highly resistant to change and devoted to short workweeks and long holidays. One consequence of neo-liberal assaults against unions is that many of those who work in the precarious sector resent full-time, unionized workers. When unionized workers go on strike, it is not difficult for the news media to find lower-paid part-time workers to complain that fat-cat union members should have to contend with the insecurities that are the lot in life of the majority. Employers have always benefited from resentments between different segments of the workforce. Today's division of the workforce into the inner segment and the precarious segment suits them to a T.

The highly diverse character of today's labour force can in effect divide workers into competitive subgroups that bear resentments against one another. Race, ethnicity, and gender are crucial lines of demarcation in the contemporary labour force. Resentments among workers on the basis of race, ethnicity, and religion are nothing new.

The history of struggles within the working class is not a pretty story to gladden the hearts of trade union militants. Resistance to immigrant workers who threaten to compete with and reduce the remuneration of the existing working force is a recurring part of the history of working people. Resentment among workers against the Chinese labourers who played a central role in constructing the railways in both Canada and the United States resulted in numerous brawls, beatings, and lynchings and led to popular support for laws restricting Chinese immigration to Canada and the United States.

The impact of the neo-liberal social model is one of the chief causes of the crash of 2008. This is because the suppression of wage and salary increases—the heart of the neo-liberal model—both in the advanced countries and throughout the world has had the inexorable effect of limiting the size of the market for goods and services and consequently for increased profits. This is the old capitalist conundrum. While individual capitalists benefit from keeping the wages and salaries they pay as low as possible, collectively they benefit from making wages and salaries as high as possible. Keeping its own wage bill low obviously directly enhances a company's profits. There is simply more left over for the shareholders or owners. Paradoxically, a company is aided if its competitors have high wage bills for the simple reason that this means there will be more money in the pockets of consumers to purchase the goods and services of firms in general, including those determined to keep their own wage bills as low as possible.

This is an insoluble dilemma. Individual firms, concerned exclusively with their own results, are not prepared to raise wage and salaries as a way of serving the general interest, including the interests of other private firms. Indeed, they only raise the wages and salaries they pay in response to effective pressure from unions or from the existence of labour shortages. They also raise wages if forced to do so as a consequence of minimum-wage legislation or of full-employment state policies that succeed in keeping the pool of surplus labour as small as possible. During the Keynesian age of the postwar decades, wages and salaries did rise for a variety of reasons. Under pressure from electorates with keen memories of the privations of the Great Depression and the war, as well as of the effectiveness of wartime economic planning, governments made job creation and full employment top priorities.

Under conditions in which the pool of surplus labour was minimal, unions undertook highly effective drives to organize the unorganized. During the postwar decades, the trade union movements reached the peak of their economic and societal influence in Western Europe, Canada, and the United States. In a period often described as a golden age, wage and salary earners achieved greater influence than ever before in the history of capitalism. Real wages rose, social programs were expanded, educational opportunities were widened. For the first time in history, the majority of wage and salary earners in the advanced countries were no longer poor.

During the period of the "great social compromise," while corporations remained at the helm in directing the economy and reaping the benefits, workers had to be taken into consideration as never before. Of critical importance to the stability of these arrangements, this was also an era of national capitalism within the framework of the U.S.-centred Bretton Woods economic system. In this period of fixed exchange rates, as opposed to the system of floating exchange rates, with which we live, the U.S. dollar was the reserve currency of the world, exchangeable for gold at a rate of U.S.$35 an ounce, and exchangeable as well for other currencies. Despite rising trade and investment abroad on the part of multinational corporations, this was also an age of national capitalism, with the state in each advanced country playing a seminal role in steering the system. It was the age of the so-called "mixed economy," a designation that acknowledged the predominant role of the private sector but also the power of the state and its responsibility to steer the economy to achieve broad objectives, the most important being full employment.

Following the intermediate decade of the 1970s, when economic storms and shocks led to the collapse of the Keynesian consensus, rising government deficits and debts, slower economic growth, and the existence of high inflation alongside high unemployment, the transition was rapid to the new age of globalization, deregulation, and neo-liberalism. The leading political stars of this new age of the right were Margaret Thatcher, elected to lead a Conservative government in Britain in 1979, and Ronald Reagan, elected president of the United States the following year.

Neo-liberalism dismantled the regulatory systems that had been in place during the postwar decades. In the Anglo-American world, and in other nations as well, the doors were thrown open to the free movement of capital internationally. National governments lost their ability to control capital flows. Gigantic new corporate investments outside the developed countries tore away at the balance of power that existed between capital and labour. Able to gain access to much cheaper labour on an enormous scale, corporations threw workers and their unions onto the defensive.

From the early 1980s to the present, corporations have been running away from labour in the advanced countries. This has weakened the viability of labour's past gains in every advanced country. For instance, in Sweden, the country in which labour arguably made the most headway in ensuring high wages and salaries, job security, effective social programs, and access to higher education, capital has managed to use the favourable conditions that flow from globalization to undermine the much touted Swedish model. To escape from the high cost of Swedish labour, Sweden's corporate giants—Ericsson, Ikea, Electrolux, the Wallenberg corporate empire, SKF, Saab, and Volvo—have shifted an ever growing proportion of their investments outside Sweden to avail themselves of cheaper labour.

The consequence is that the power once held by Swedish labour in relation to Swedish capital has diminished. The proportion of Swedish wage and salary earners who are members of unions—once as high as 90 per cent—has declined. While the large majority of Swedish workers remain unionized, the effectiveness of nation-wide bargaining with the corporations is not what it once was. Furthermore, Swedish membership in the European Union (EU) has furthered this process. While EU wages and salaries, employment benefits, and job security provisions are better than those in Canada and the United States, they are not as advanced as those in Sweden. Swedes, as a consequence, are being pulled in the direction of the EU model.

In other advanced countries, the consequences of globalization have been more dramatic for wage and salary earners. In the United States and Canada the income of the average worker, adjusted for inflation, has remained about the same over the past quarter-century. In the United States, only 12 per cent of employees were unionized in 2006; in Canada, the proportion was much higher at 31.4 per cent in 2007, but the numbers too have been declining.[5] The same trends were evident in Britain in the years after Thatcher was first elected in 1979.

While the Anglo-American world, including Canada, has given itself over to neo-liberalism with few hesitations, that cannot be said to have been the case for continental Western Europe. In France and Germany, a much more state-centred socio-economic model, sometimes called the Westphalian model, has established priorities that differ from those encountered in the Anglo-American model. Especially in France, the state has worked closely with the private sector and at times with labour to establish broad economic goals for the economy, in a system of "indicative" planning, a term used to distinguish French planning from the command economy and centralized planning of the former Soviet Union. In the Federal Republic of Germany, the goal has been to sustain what Germany's constitution calls a "social market" economy. In this economy, free enterprise must work within the framework of the right of labour to co-determine the direction of corporations and the economy. While private capital is dominant, labour's role is spelt out in the Federal Republic's constitution and in the relationship between corporations and unions. In both the French and German versions of the model, it is much more difficult to lay off workers than is the case in the Anglo-American model. Companies laying off permanent employees have to pay severance amounting to up to a year's wages.

Anglo-American neo-liberalism has had a major impact on capitalism everywhere, including the capitalism of France and Germany. For the past quarter-century, U.S. and British economists and entrepreneurs have been telling the continental Europeans that they need to modernize their economies by making their labour markets more flexible. They have used the success of countries such as Ireland in moving over to the new model—Ireland has now been much more deeply devastated by the crash of 2008 than France and Germany have been—to make the case. Under pressure to adopt a more Anglo-American style of capitalism, not least from within from politicians such as Nicolas Sarkozy, elected president of France in 2007, continental Europe has moved in the direction of neo-liberalism. Among other things, employers in France have strongly preferred to hire part-timers rather than full-timers over the past couple of decades. Part-timers can be paid less and they can be laid off more cheaply.

Even in Japan, with its own very distinct brand of capitalism, the pressures of Anglo-American liberalism have been considerable. Especially during the 1980s, the Japanese model was widely touted as superior to that of the United States. From the early 1960s to the end of the 1980s, Japan's rate of economic growth was much stronger than that in the United States, and Japan's industrial prowess in the auto industry, electronics, machinery, steel, and robotics reinforced the prestige of Japanese capitalism. In 1986 Japan replaced the United States as the world's leading creditor nation, while the United States plunged into a condition of ever greater net indebtedness. Japanese labour was renowned for its work ethic, an outcome that analysts explained as resulting from the tendency of Japanese employers to consult workers much more than their counterparts elsewhere consulted their own employees. In addition, Japanese companies such as Toyota and Sony were famed for their long-term product development. Engineers played a much bigger role in Japanese capitalism than was the case in the United States, where companies were run by accountants and managers with their eye on a short-term return on investment from quarter to quarter. These conditions explain the rise of Toyota and the fall of General Motors.

What took the glow off the Japanese model was the implosion of the real estate bubble that was centred on Japan at the end of the 1980s. The crash of real estate values, especially in Japan, but very widely throughout the world, dragged down Japanese financial institutions that were deeply invested in real estate. Japan's financial meltdown (often compared with the 2008 U.S. meltdown) and a wave of corruption scandals implicating government officials have held the Japanese economy back ever since. This did not mean the end of Japanese industrial success—Toyota occupies a much more enviable place in the world today than General Motors does—but the slowed pace of Japanese economic growth and the prestige of the Anglo-American model during the high-tech years of the 1990s placed pressure on Japan to adopt elements of the neoliberal economic model. Since then Japan has responded to some extent to the call for less government economic intervention and the end of the "job for life" career pattern for permanent workers employed by the major companies.

While the continental European and Japanese models have remained distinct, Anglo-American capitalism has dominated, and its modus operandi has been adopted at least in part by capitalists everywhere.

How then has the neo-liberal model played a key role in triggering the crash?

The widening divide between a tiny minority at the top, especially in the Anglo-American world, and the rest of the population has limited the growth of the market for goods and services. When those at the top keep too much for themselves and hold wages and salaries down, they set themselves up for an economic crisis. The same was true in the 1920s on the eve of the crash of 1929. This time, the financial capitalists who were at the centre of the meltdown spent the first decade of this new century trying to stave off the crisis—in the aftermath of the bursting of the dot.com bubble—with a whole series of new initiatives in the realm of subprime mortgages, in the promotion of personal debt, and in the sale of a long list of financial products under the headings of securitization, credit default swaps, and other derivatives. The heavy indebtedness created in this venture would have lethal consequences.

Chapter Seven

AMERICAN DEBT

AND THE GLOBAL CRISIS

———————

IN SHARP CONTRAST to the Great Depression of the 1930s, when it was the world's leading creditor nation, the United States is now the greatest debtor in the world. This dubious standing places enormous constraints on the course that the country can pursue in attempts to cope with the economic crisis and the broader foreign challenges that confront it. Of particularly importance to the external position of the United States are two financial issues: the government deficit and debt; and the current account deficit.

By mid-2009 the U.S. national debt amounted to the unfathomable figure of U.S.$11 trillion and was set to soar much higher. The Obama administration's economic recovery plan was driving the government's annual deficit from U.S.$410 billion at the beginning of 2008 to well over a trillion dollars a year. The administration projected that trillion-dollar deficits would persist for years to come. The federal debt is financed in part by securities held by U.S. government accounts; among the most important are the

Federal Employees Retirement Funds and the Federal Old-Age and Survivors Insurance Trust Fund. At the beginning of 2008, 55 per cent of the debt was held by the "public," meaning those who purchased U.S. treasury bonds. Some 45 per cent of these "public" purchases were made by foreigners, with two-thirds of that total by foreign central banks. By far the most important of these clients were the central banks of China and Japan. Indeed, the central banks of China and Japan and other purchasers from those two countries made about 47 per cent of the total purchases by foreigners.[1] In all, foreigners have financed about 25 per cent of the gigantic U.S. national debt, and the Obama agenda could drive that percentage much higher.

Between them, the central banks of China and Japan hold over a trillion dollars' worth of the U.S. securities used to finance the U.S. national debt. These banks do not buy the securities because they regard them as a good investment: quite the contrary. They buy them in effect to save the United States from the crippling consequences of its own internal weakness. This they do not as an act of generosity, but to safeguard their own vitally important export markets in the United States and thereby prevent a global economic collapse. Suppose the Chinese and Japanese central banks, along with about eight or ten other central banks, decided to reduce their purchases of U.S. treasury bonds. The consequence would be a sharp decline in the value of the U.S. dollar against other currencies. A lower dollar would lead to a substantial reduction of U.S. imports. Keeping exports flowing into the vast U.S. market is what motivates Asian central bankers to buy trillions of dollars' worth of U.S. treasury bonds.

This willingness to serve as lenders for the deeply indebted Americans has its limits. The biggest money-makers in China are foreign multinational corporations that set up shop in that country to avail themselves of a highly productive and relatively inexpensive labour force. Those multinationals earn a far higher return on their invested capital in China than the Chinese central bank makes in sustaining the U.S. dollar through its purchases of U.S. treasury bonds. In March 2009 the Chinese central bank issued a clear warning that it was tiring of playing such a pivotal role in propping up the U.S. dollar. Zhou Xiaochuan, the governor of the People's Bank of China, suggested that the time had come to consider replacing the dollar as a global reserve currency with a new currency made up of a basket of currencies, to include the euro, yen, pound, and dollar. Zhou proposed that the International Monetary Fund (IMF) increase the use of "Special Drawing Rights," a notional currency (not available for regular transactions) already used by the IMF.[2] Not surprisingly, both President Obama and U.S. Treasury Secretary Timothy Geithner rejected the Chinese idea and predicted that the dollar would remain the world's dominant reserve currency for a long time to come.

The Obama administration will need to sell vastly more treasury bonds—perhaps more than double the 2009 dollar total—to Asian and other central bankers, which will, for one thing, substantially increase the downward pressure on the U.S. dollar against other currencies. A renewed fall in the value of the U.S. dollar will serve as yet another disincentive in the path of central bankers and private investors buying up the bonds. Buying bonds denominated in a falling currency is a money-loser, especially if the interest rates on the bonds are low. To sweeten the pot, the U.S. government will have to substantially raise the interest rates on its treasury bonds, both to slow the decline in its dollar and to increase the return to the buyers of the bonds.

This process creates yet another problem for the United States. Higher interest rates on U.S. bonds make the cost of financing the rapidly expanding U.S. national debt ever more dauntingly stratospheric. Thus, borrowing immensely more from foreigners to finance the administration's stimulus program is an exercise that can only be described as fraught. The more expensive the cost of borrowing, the less effective will be the recovery program.

In principle there is a way of reducing the volume of additional foreign borrowing. It could be done by dramatically reducing the income and wealth gaps between the rich and the rest of the U.S. population, in part by imposing much higher income and wealth taxes on the very affluent. While in theory this strategy could work, in practice it would necessitate such an enormous shift in the American socio-economic system that it is inconceivable under present circumstances. Thus it remains only a theoretical possibility. The continuing dependence of the United States on foreign borrowing, and thus on the need to tie much of the world into an American-centred geopolitical system, is rooted in the marked inequality that exists in the United States itself.

Adding to the problem is the U.S. current account deficit, which by spring 2009 was running at an annual rate of U.S.$673 billion.[3] To finance this gigantic current account deficit, which amounts to just under 5 per cent of the U.S. Gross Domestic Product of $14.3 trillion, the country is forced to engage in immense foreign borrowing, which can take a number of forms. One of the most important is the inflow of investments by foreigners to acquire assets in the United States. During the 1990s these inflows were occurring at a time when the United States was on the cutting edge of the global technological revolution—the age of the dot.com boom. Following the dot.com crash in 2000, though, much of the flow of new foreign equity into the United States halted. Indeed, in coming years, if the U.S. dollar should drop significantly against other currencies, foreign investment inflows into the United States would most likely be aimed at the acquisition, on the cheap, of U.S. economic assets. This is hardly a prospect that the government and corporate sector can view with equanimity.

For any country to have a perennial current account deficit that runs at just under 5 per cent of its GDP is a perilous exercise. For any country other than the United States to do it is unthinkable. The United States—as those who believe that America can go on running this deficit indefinitely insist—has a special role in the global system that gives it the privilege of greater indebtedness than other countries are allowed. Among other reasons for this position is the continuing role of the U.S. dollar as the reserve currency of the world. What this means is that when the U.S. government borrows money abroad it does so in its own currency. Thus, even if that currency depreciates against other currencies, Washington does not have to assume the additional cost that such depreciation would impose on other borrowing governments.

The merit of this argument has declined as the prospects for the further depreciation of the U.S. dollar have increased. The burden to be borne by foreign central banks has simply grown dangerously large, and it is about to become more enormous still.

The U.S. current account deficit—the extent to which the United States spends more abroad than it earns abroad—creates a paradoxical situation for the United States in its relationships with other countries. On the one hand, China, Japan, and other countries, including Canada, depend heavily on the vast U.S. market for the profitability of the enterprises based on their soil. It might help to picture the size of the U.S. market for foreigners this way: each year, as a consequence of its current account deficit, the United States offers to foreign suppliers an additional market that is more than half the size of the entire Canadian market. This market exists on top of what the U.S. market could offer foreigners if Americans sold abroad as much as they bought. The paradox is that foreigners have to pay dearly to keep this market open and available to them. The bigger the U.S. current account deficit, the more lucrative the market is to foreigners. But the bigger the current account deficit, the more burdensome is the weight of the unprofitable U.S. treasury bonds that foreigners must buy to keep that market open.

An inherent instability is at work here. It is the kind of arrangement that could only exist in the relationship between a declining empire, or hegemon, and its clients. When the United States was a rising empire—as it was even in the dark days of the Great Depression of the 1930s—its creditor status, its superior productive plants, and ultimately its unexcelled military potential ensured its ability to invest abroad on its own terms and to dictate its trade arrangements with other countries. Indeed, in the last days of the Second World War, in the summer of 1944, the United States, along with its allies, established the rudiments of the postwar economic system at Bretton Woods, New Hampshire, placing itself at the centre.

At what point will foreigners conclude that the game is not worth the candle, that financing the floundering United States is more trouble than it is worth? With so many factors at play, including the stresses so evident in the U.S. effort to sustain its geostrategic position in the world, no precise answer can be given to this exceptionally important question. What is abundantly clear, however, is that the Asian powers and the Europeans could adopt economic strategies in which the role of the United States as a market of necessity (much more for the Asians than the Europeans) becomes far less important than it is today.

———————

Every winter, government and business high-flyers from around the world flock to Davos, Switzerland, to pontificate about the state of the world economy. In January 2009 the World Economic Forum at Davos was unusually subdued. Those who ran the global economy were not receiving high kudos from anyone about the job they had been doing.

A major topic at Davos in 2009 was how the Obama administration was going to raise the U.S.$819 billion it was seeking to finance its stimulus package. Unprecedented borrowing of capital from foreigners would be needed to fund the program. Experts at Davos warned that U.S. borrowing could push up interest rates, generate inflation, and drive down the value of the U.S. dollar against other currencies. While some might wonder about the risk of inflation in a global setting in which deflation, its opposite, posed the greater peril, the question of where the capital would come from was on many minds. Alan S. Blinder, a Princeton University economist and former vice-chairman of the Federal Reserve in Washington, told *The New York Times*: "At some point, there may be so much Treasury debt that investors may start wondering if they are overloaded in dollar assets."[4] Another concern raised at Davos—and a concern expressed many times in recent years—was that U.S. borrowing would have the effect of making it extremely difficult for poorer countries to borrow the capital they urgently require. Ernesto Zedillo, the former Mexican president who was in office during his country's financial crisis in 1994, warned: "The U.S. needs to show some proof they have a plan to get out of the fiscal problem. We, as developing countries, need to know we won't be crowded out of the capital markets, which is already happening."[5]

While much of the focus, and rightly so, has been on U.S. public debt and the gargantuan U.S. current account deficit, the equally alarming level of U.S. private debt has enormous implications for the prospects for economic recovery in the United States. In 1960 the household debt of Americans stood at a level that was equivalent to 50 per cent of the U.S. GDP. By 1980 that level had grown to 60 per cent of U.S. GDP. Since 1980 the level of household debt in the United States has reached unprecedented levels. By 2004 the average American was spending U.S.$1.04 for every $1.00 he or she earned. By the end of that year consumer debt alone (not all of household debt) had reached an amount equivalent to 85.7 per cent of U.S. GDP.[6]

There are various ways of analyzing the shocking rise of U.S. private debt. Some see it as a cultural phenomenon, the consequence of the inability of contemporary Americans to defer gratification. Others attribute sky-high consumer debt to the mass marketing of credit cards and the goods and travel that flow from the cards. Campaigns to win over young Americans to credit card use have been especially effective. Between 1990 and 2003 the number of Americans holding credit cards jumped from 82 million to 144 million.[7] A fundamental cause of the rise of personal indebtedness has to do with the stagnation of the incomes of most Americans since 1980. An economy in which the mass of the population enjoys rises in real incomes is one in which the market for goods and service expands rapidly; but an economy in which incomes for the majority are stagnant is one in which real barriers stand in the way of market expansion. Just as they found ways of expanding the markets for their activities by promoting mortgages and home purchases to millions of people who could not afford them, financial institutions were enormously successful in enticing tens of millions of Americans to spend today, building up massive debts for the future.

Now the time has come to pay the piper, and that is no easy task. Now that Humpty Dumpty has fallen, even Obama's vigour, intelligence, and dedication may not be enough to put the pieces back together again. The problem is that the crash in the United States occurred when the financial institutions, with the full support of Washington, had used up every method they could think of to grind more profits for themselves out of the system. What they had created was an arrangement with distinct similarities to a gigantic Ponzi scheme. A full-fledged Ponzi scheme exists when a financier like Bernie Madoff takes the money of investors, promises them a high rate of return, and then pays them dividends not drawn from profits but from the capital invested by the next group of investors. While U.S. financiers had not created a pyramid scheme along the lines of Madoff's, they had erected a system that was constructed on vast layers of debt. If the economy stopped moving forward, a crash, when it came, would create vicious cycles involving all those layers of debt.

That is what happened with the crash of 1929. When the market fell, it forced all those who had made investments on margin to sell off the positions they held to pay off the margin calls they had to meet. This pulled the market down much further. The system was running in reverse. The same thing happened with the crash of 2008. The ways in which leverage was exercised in the twenty-first century were much more arcane and technologically advanced than the old method of stock purchases on margin of the 1920s. But through a slew of derivatives and other financial instruments, the same result was achieved. With the investment of, let's say, U.S.$1 million, high rollers, whether individuals or enormous financial firms, were able to achieve the leverage of an investment of as much as $30 million. Such leverage yielded huge profits. But the crash put a halt to the whole machine. Individuals and enormous companies such as AIG were unable to cover their positions. Left exposed, they plunged into bankruptcy. Too big to fail, Washington rushed in to save the giants. First the Bush administration and then the Obama administration tried desperately to put Humpty Dumpty back together again.

The problem with Humpty Dumpty, the financial sector of the American economy, is that while Washington believed it was too big to be allowed to fail, it had actually grown too big to succeed.

———

Over the past quarter-century an extraordinary shift has occurred in the makeup of the U.S. economy. As late as the early 1980s, manufacturing accounted for close to 20 per cent of the economy, while the financial sector (commercial banking, investment banking, insurance firms, and other financial firms) generated 12 to 14 per cent of GDP. By the eve of the 2008 crash, manufacturing had shrunk to 12 per cent of GDP while finance had swollen to account for 20 to 21 per cent of GDP.[8]

That over one-fifth of the economic output of a major nation— we are not talking about the Cayman Islands or even Switzerland— is accounted for by finance is a shocking phenomenon. Considering the allure that finance had acquired in the English-speaking countries by the eve of the crash, it is not surprising that analysts rarely step back to consider what this really means. In theory at least, finance is not a benign phenomenon in and of itself. It is a means to an end. The proper and most efficacious raising and investing of capital are supposed to open the way for the production of goods and services that are actually useful to, or desired by, people—that is, manufactured goods, food, houses, education, medical care, entertainment, a host of other services, and transportation.

On its own, finance is not useful to people. Only as a means to an end does it have value in any meaningful sense of the word. In a great and powerful country such as the United States, once the world's leading industrial nation, when manufacturing steadily shrinks and finance expands remorselessly as a proportion of GDP, we have to ask ourselves what is really going on.

One thing that has been going on is that a few people have been vastly enriched by the immense profits juiced out of the engorged financial sector. These are the people who have now become notorious, in the aftermath of the crash, for their sky-high salaries, advantageous stock options, and gargantuan bonuses. As finance became a huge industry unto itself, more and more of the "best and the brightest" among the young eschewed engineering, medicine, scientific research, and other fields to go into "money."

On campuses across North America, universities have responded to the rise of "money" as an industry by establishing schools of business whose function is to turn out graduates ready and eager to work in the financial sector. Money has been sexy; manufacturing has been old hat. At business schools a very particular school of economics has dominated the curriculum. Students are taught how to apply neo-classical economics in the setting of contemporary globalization. In the world view as they receive it, free trade is benign, as is the right to invest anywhere in the world and to shift investments freely from country to country. Protectionism is a negative condition, and so too are government interference in economic decision-making and militant trade unionism. Other schools of economics get short shrift at business schools, which are also not enamoured with having their students take courses from academic departments that more thoroughly critique neo-classical economics. It is no exaggeration to say that the economics taught to business students in North America fits hand and glove with the economic practices that have been found so wanting in the aftermath of the crash of 2008.

Of more immediate concern is whether the Obama administration remains hooked on a finance-centred conception of the economy. Over the past couple of decades, as finance has grown ever larger as a proportion of the GDP, financial institutions have evolved a plethora of instruments, more or less arcane, whose purpose is to invite investors to heighten the risk, or the pleasure, that flows from their investments. Among the products on the market, investors could choose from securitization, credit default swaps, and derivatives in many shapes and sizes. Securitization is a process that creates instruments that enable those who have lent money to sell the loans—credit-card debts, sub-prime mortgages, car loans, for instance—to those who want to purchase these instruments as investments. The idea, of course, is to spread risk widely, so that investors assume a portion of the risk, leaving the way open to make a healthy return when times are good. "Banks used securitization to increase their risk," wrote Paul Krugman in *The New York Times*, "not reduce it, and in the process they made the economy more, not less, vulnerable to financial disruption. Sooner or later, things were bound to go wrong, and eventually they did. Bear Stearns failed; Lehman failed; but most of all, securitization failed."[9] In October 2008 Columbia University economics professor Joseph Stiglitz quipped to a congressional committee in Washington, "Securitization was based on the premise that a fool was born every minute."[10] The problem with securitization, as with other exotic instruments, was that while the spreading of risk allowed financial institutions to do yet more lending to increase their risk, when the market plummeted the investments under the securitization label blew up, became toxic, and helped drag their holders towards bankruptcy.

Credit default swaps were another Alice in Wonderland creation that apparently provided protection for investors, but actually vanished into inutility just when the insurance they supposedly provided was actually needed. As the name suggests, credit default swaps involve a deal between two parties: a swap in which one party is buying protection and the other party is selling protection. They are betting on whether a particular company will default on its bonds. The first party is buying protection so that if the company does default within a specified period of time, it will collect a large payment from the party selling the protection. The second party, the seller, receives payments for assuming the risk. Thus the purchaser of the credit default swap is acquiring what looks like an insurance policy; the protection covers the purchaser, who can then go out and make other risky investments without the appearance of having a balance sheet that involves too much risk. The seller collects money for selling protection on, let's say, a risky bond in the sub-prime mortgage market. In recent years, according to some estimates, hundreds of *trillions* of dollars of these credit swaps have been made. The numbers involved are absurdly large. For comparison, the U.S. GDP is about U.S.$14 trillion.

In the run-up to the great crash of 2008, credit default swaps were traded in the creation of an ever higher fantasy skyscraper. When the sub-prime mortgage market, among others, imploded, the entities that had sold credit default swaps suddenly discovered that the assets they held on them were reduced to rubble. In March 2008, after Moody's downgraded its ratings, Bear Stearns—the party involved in U.S.$13 billion in credit default swap trades— imploded and was acquired for next to nothing by J.P. Morgan.

No one knows how huge the bill could be for the collapse of the credit default gambit. That is because with hundreds of trillions of notional dollars gambled in the various forms of exotic financial instruments, including credit default swaps, it is next to impossible to calculate the price tag for the potential collapse of it all. The Bank for International Settlements (BIS), an international organization of central banks based in Basel, Switzerland, took a crack at calculating the potential risk, making use of 2007 data. The BIS estimated the notional value of the whole at U.S.$596 trillion, divided among interest rate derivatives ($393 trillion), credit default swaps ($58 trillion), and currency derivatives ($56 trillion), with the rest allocated to other categories. The BIS calculated that the net risk from all of this was U.S.$14.5 trillion, and the gross credit exposure was $3.256 trillion.[11]

The utility of such calculations is questionable. What we learn from this sort of abstract exercise is the vastness of these shadowy transactions, which can and do have implications for the real world. To make sense of this, we need to understand the motivation underlying the proliferation of exotic financial instruments, and more broadly what caused their emergence. This takes us back to our discussion about the predominance of the neo-liberal Anglo-American model in the world. Holding down the growth in real wages and salaries has limited the expansion of the market for goods and services. In response, the financial sector has proliferated enormously, with the motivation being the rapacious quest for new sources of profits. In our time, capitalism has cannibalized itself. The financial sector has grown ever larger as a proportion of U.S. GDP—not to produce useful goods and services, but to squeeze ever more out of the existing economic pie.

Pushing out sub-prime mortgages to people who often could not afford them, and credit cards to millions of people who then maxed out their cards, and introducing financial products to heighten the leverage of investors: these have all been ways in which finance could juice out more profits for itself. Most of that activity has involved various forms of borrowing against the future. Today's capitalism, swollen with debts that will take many years to reduce or write off, has fouled its own future, ensuring lean years ahead.

As is the case in its most extreme form with a Ponzi scheme, the cannibalizing of the economy by financial institutions has shifted the economic engine into reverse. Now that the time has come to cope with the debts, both the toxic and the more salubrious ones, the impact of the activities of financial institutions has been to put the brakes on the economy for coming years. The same thing happened with the financial meltdown of 1929, when the world of buying on margin imploded.

Just over two months after Obama was sworn into office, the United States seethed with populist rage. Storm clouds had been forming ever since the bailouts of financial firms began in the fall of 2008, when the Bush administration was still in office. What caused this maelstrom were the payments of bonuses totalling U.S.$165 million to executives of the American International Group in March 2009, in the wake of Washington's massive bailout of AIG, which amounted to more than U.S.$170 billion. Everywhere across the country, ordinary Americans were furious. With rising anxiety they had numbly accepted the vast Wall Street bailouts and the talk of trillions of more dollars needed to get the financial sector and the auto industry back in business. But the idea of the people who had presided over the AIG plunge into toxicity receiving handouts of a million dollars each, and in some cases more, blew the lid off.

I was in California when the hurricane hit. On television, on the front pages of papers in small and large cities, in conversations in cafés, the fury was everywhere. CNN covered a busload of working people, some of them political activists, going on a tour of the palatial homes owned by AIG executives, to deliver the message to the doorstep that they were angry. They were met by security guards who halted them and so delivered the message to the Pinkerton police. CNN titled the segment "The Lives of the Rich and Shameless."

American populism extends from left to right. As has been the case for decades, when it rears its head populism can be anti-capitalist one moment, and racist the next. It can demand fairness for all one day, and then recoil in fury against the guy next door who is living on the dole. During the Great Depression of the 1930s, populism showed up under the banners of the Congress of Industrial

Organizations (CIO), with its drive to unionize industrial workers, of Louisiana's Huey Long, as well as of the fascistic Father Charles Coughlin. That man, Coughlin, was adept at sounding radical, as when he urged his audience to "attack and overpower the enemy of financial slavery."

In the United Kingdom, when banks crashed in the autumn of 2008, the government of Prime Minister Gordon Brown did not hesitate to nationalize them. The pumping of capital into these banks was accompanied by government control and public equity. If the banks returned to profitability while they remained in the hands of the Crown, the public would earn a return on its investment. In the United States, the ideological recoil from the very idea of nationalizing banks was much stronger. It amounted to a violation against the very shibboleths on which U.S. capitalism rested, a step that was to be avoided unless there was absolutely no alternative. The Obama administration, as Krugman observed, appeared "to be tying itself in knots" to avoid having taxpayers take ownership in return for their rescue of banks. The dilemma that Krugman noted was that "bank stocks are worth so little these days— Citigroup and Bank of America have a combined market value of only $52 billion—that the ownership wouldn't be partial: pumping in enough taxpayer money to make the banks sound would, in effect, turn them into publicly owned enterprises."[12]

The problem for Obama was that many of his top officials were deeply involved with Wall Street. Treasury Secretary Geithner, to name one prominent case, was a Wall Street enabler for years. Mentored by Clinton-era treasury secretaries Robert Rubin and Lawrence Summers, Geithner was named president of the Federal Reserve Bank of New York in 2003. He was critically involved in the sale of Bear Stearns, in the bailout of AIG, and in the decision to let Lehman Brothers go down. He was the principal architect of the Obama administration's move to partner up with the private sector to buy up the toxic assets of Wall Street financial firms.

While right-wing populist ranters such as Rush Limbaugh salivate about the evils of big government, there is nothing that big financial firms and other top corporations love more than handouts of tax dollars to them. The Obama administration's policy towards the financial sector, in his first months in office, was to shovel out the money while leaving the private bankers in charge. The president was so afraid of nationalizing the banks that he was willing to run the risk of putting Wall Street back in the driver's seat while leaving the taxpayers stuck with a mountain of bad debts.

As soon as Bush was out of the White House and Obama in, the Republicans turned their guns on the size of the stimulus package being proposed and on the danger of government control of the economy. Even in the last months of the Bush administration, the White House had to rely on the Democrats to push through its bailouts of the financial sector. Out of power in the executive branch and both houses of Congress, the Republicans became the defenders of tax cuts. They pushed for new tax incentives to lure buyers back into the housing market, argued for smaller government, and warned Americans of the perils of socialism.

In *The New York Times*, columnist Frank Rich wrote:

> The Republicans do have one idea, of course, but it's hardly fresh: more and bigger tax cuts, particularly for business and the well-off. That's the sum of their "alternative" stimulus plan. Obama has tried to accommodate this panacea, perhaps to a fault. Mainstream economists in both parties believe that tax

cuts in the stimulus package will deliver far less bang for the buck than, say, infrastructure spending. The tax-cut stimulus embraced a year ago by the G.O.P. induced next-to-no consumer spending as Americans merely banked the savings or paid down debt.[13]

Even in opposition, the political right, which speaks for much of U.S. business, has had a significant impact on the national debate. In a country in which socialism is a dirty word and free enterprise is a deity, the Obama administration has bent over backwards to avoid the appearance of promoting a government takeover of the U.S. banking system.

In January 2009, as the Obama administration weighed the idea of an immense new bailout of the banking system, Treasury Secretary Geithner declared, "We have a financial system that is run by private shareholders, managed by private institutions, and we'd like to do our best to preserve that system."[14] Obama's much touted promise to transcend the partisan divide forced his administration to cut U.S.$80 billion from his economic stimulus package. The cuts came in plans to spend money on school construction, on aid to the unemployed to maintain their health care, and in the provision of food stamps, among other things. In return for these cuts to his plan, the president failed to win the support of a single Republican in the House of Representatives. He wound up with the backing of only a handful of Republican Senators.

Potential public backlash against the stimulus package and especially against additional measures to bail out financial institutions posed yet more risks for the administration. The Bush administration's U.S.$700 billion bailout of the financial sector in autumn

2008—half of which had been paid out under the Troubled Asset Relief Program by the time Obama took office—was deeply unpopular with the American people. As President Obama sought to win public and congressional support for his stimulus package, he struck out at the practice of handing out huge bonuses to executives at Wall Street firms that were surviving on infusions of public money. The announcement that in 2008, the worst year since the Great Depression for Wall Street, firms handed out over U.S.$18 billion in executive bonuses brought the issue to a head. Obama said that at a time when the economy was faltering and Washington was spending billions to keep Wall Street firms afloat, such bonuses were "shameful." In an interview with NBC Nightly News the president said, "If taxpayers are helping you, then you have certain responsibilities to not be living high on the hog."

On February 4 Obama and Geithner announced that in firms receiving significant funds from Washington, executive compensation would be capped at U.S.$500,000 a year. To put this sum in perspective, Obama's annual salary as president of the United States is U.S.$400,000. But to top Wall Street CEOs, half a million dollars a year is chump change. In 2007 the top guns at Wall Street firms were compensated at a much more stratospheric level. John Thain of Merrill Lynch took home U.S.$83 million; Lloyd Blankfein of Goldman Sachs, $54 million; Kenneth Chenault of American Express, $51.7 million; and John Mack of Morgan Stanley, $41.7 million.

To the average American, half a million dollars sounded like a great deal of money. To top corporate executives it was a meagre ration. James Reda, the founder and managing director of James F. Reda and Associates, a compensation-consulting firm, thought the pay cap would not work. "That is pretty draconian—$500,000 is not a lot of money," he said, "particularly if there is no bonus." Reda said that few large companies pay their top executives such puny salaries and that it would be "really tough to get people to staff" corporations if they have to apply such a cap. Reda was among those warning that top executive talent would flee to firms that were not being bailed out by Washington and therefore were not subject to such a miserably low salary cap.

The question of compensation has always been a tricky one in the United States. According to the American Dream, earning an enormous income and acquiring great wealth are among the rewards possible for anyone with the drive, imagination, and luck to make it. Nothing should ever stand in the way of this dream being fulfilled, according to the American creed. But with the crash of Wall Street's titanic firms, CEOs and top executives of the bailed-out firms became the butt of the harsh populist humour of Americans.

It is a cardinal error to believe that the United States will sustain its present role at the centre of the global economy and that it can continue the virtually unlimited access to foreign borrowing that it has enjoyed in recent decades. Although this is a reality that has not been widely acknowledged in public discourse, the United States will have to navigate a wrenching economic transition. One cost that is virtually certain to accompany this change of direction is a falling standard of living for the American people.

Chapter Eight

THE HOUSE THE

NEO - LIBERALS BUILT

———————

THE ECONOMIC SYSTEM that now lies in ruins—the neo-liberal system—rose out of the ashes of the Keynesian arrangements that prevailed during the postwar decades. The rise and demise of the postwar mixed economy, whose patron saint was John Maynard Keynes, was the historical backdrop for the construction of the neo-liberal order, whose patron saint was Milton Friedman.

In Western Europe and North America, the late 1940s to early 1970s was a remarkable period that came to be seen in subsequent decades as a golden age. Unlike other eras, whose hallmark was war or the rise of new global centres of power, this was the age whose signature feature was the improving well-being of the average person. While the details differed from country to country, what was common throughout the advanced countries was a strikingly new condition: for the first time in history the majority of the population in these regions were rising above the mean status of being poor.

While the early postwar years were difficult for working people in Western Europe, that situation changed as a consequence of what were called economic miracles in West Germany in the 1950s and France and Italy in the 1960s. Conditions in Britain also generally improved as a result of slow progress, the end of rationing, and rising wages.

The specific models differed from country to country. France, Italy, and West Germany experimented with state intervention and the participation of workers in corporate management. The planning techniques that these countries used in their own economies became crucially important in the launching of the European Common market, which over the decades grew into today's European Union.

The French four-year plans were not at all like the five-year plans in the Soviet Union, where planning meant a command economy. In France the planning was indicative: goals were set; business, the state, and unions (until unions decided to drop out of the process) kept those goals in mind in the decisions they made.

One element of the French model that would be unintelligible in the age of privatization that was to come was the deliberate use of government-owned corporations as sparkplugs to enhance the growth of productivity. During the postwar decades in France and Italy planners assumed that publicly owned companies could outperform their private-sector rivals. The showpiece example in France was Renault, the automaker. During the war, Renault's top management had collaborated with the German occupiers, and as a consequence the post-liberation government nationalized the firm. Renault's plant at Betancourt in a Paris suburb became the substance and symbol of French industrial might. It also became the symbol of working-class power, the bastion of the CGT, the national trade union congress with close ties to the Communist Party. The comparatively well paid Renault workers were pacesetters who led the way to higher wages for industrial workers across the country.

In Britain, within weeks of Germany's surrender the electorate voted Winston Churchill out of office in favour of the Labour Party led by Clement Attlee. In office with a majority in the House of Commons for the first time, Labour eschewed the most radical elements of its program, which had promised the eradication of capitalism. Attlee's government did nationalize important sectors of the economy, including the coal and steel industries and railways. But the wealthy owners of these industries used the capital acquired from the government buyouts to invest in other more dynamic businesses. The Labour Party's relative timidity was best demonstrated by the government's failure to abolish Britain's independent or private schools, a pillar of the country's class-divided society. During the postwar years the mainly upper-class graduates of Eton, Rugby, Harrow, and the others went on to Oxford and Cambridge universities and continued to win a disproportionately high number of the top positions in British society.

What Labour did do—and this transformed British society— was establish a welfare state, which included old age pensions and the widespread provision of housing built by the state. At the centre of the program was the National Health Service (NHS).

Aneurin (Nye) Bevan, the health minister who presided over the creation of the NHS, was the most radical member of the Labour cabinet. A self-educated Welshman, the son and grandson of coal miners, Bevan was determined to create a system of health care that would allow people, for the first time in history, to get access to care without first signing a cheque. The Labour government nationalized Britain's hospitals and brought general practitioners, specialists, dentists, and nurses within the NHS. Bevan made one concession to the powerful and politically conservative medical profession—a move that offended the most left-wing members of his party. Under the NHS, doctors were permitted to continue their private practices, in addition to working for the new state-managed system. This meant that many of Britain's leading specialists, among them the famed Harley Street physicians, continued to serve their wealthiest patients privately, and that the well-heeled could continue to jump the queue in getting access to the best practitioners without having to wait their turn under the public system.[1]

Many other countries, including Canada, modelled universal health-care systems on the NHS. In Canada the Liberal government of William Lyon Mackenzie King began the creation of a welfare state that owed much to the British example. The universal family allowance came first, to be followed over the years by government payment for hospital care, the Canada Pension Plan, medicare, improved unemployment insurance, and large-scale federal funding of provincial social assistance programs.

In the United States, the Truman, Eisenhower, Kennedy, and Johnson administrations were built on the foundation established by Franklin Roosevelt, whose social security system remained the most important element in the country's welfare state. The drive to achieve equal rights for racial minorities constituted the other major thrust of the postwar U.S. effort to overcome discrimination and poverty. The Supreme Court's 1954 ban of racial segregation in public schools was followed in the 1960s by legislation that banned discrimination in public accommodation, guaranteed the vote to African Americans in the South, and established affirmative action programs that provided educational and employment opportunities for minorities.

During the golden decades in the advanced countries, large industrial corporations, whether publicly or privately owned, passed on a portion of increased profits and productivity gains to workers in the form of higher wages and improved benefits. It was this model, in France, the United States, and other advanced countries, that economist John Kenneth Galbraith depicted as constituting the "new industrial state."[2] As Galbraith conceived it, the key to these large corporations in what he called the "planning sphere" was not whether they were publicly or privately owned. Such oligopolistic corporations were strongly placed to set their own prices and therefore to control the rate of return on their invested capital.

Top managers, not owners, were the key source of power in these companies, Galbraith concluded. The key objective of the managers, in his view, was to keep their mighty corporate vessels on course, in equilibrium—and not to realize the highest possible profits.

The Canadian-born Galbraith had learned his economics in unorthodox ways that led him to see things differently than colleagues who were classical economists. His first training in economics was at the Ontario Agricultural College in Guelph (now the University of Guelph), where the emphasis was on maximizing the well-being of farmers and agricultural output within a system of supply management. This background served him well when he departed for the United States to pursue his extraordinary career. The young economist served during the Second World War as deputy head of the Office of Price Administration, which gave him immense authority over the wartime system of wage and price controls and supply management for the entire U.S. economy. Unlike the classical economists, he understood first-hand what planning could achieve.

Galbraith's work was highly prized during the golden decades. In his own way he was the disciple of the greatest economist to shape the postwar decades, John Maynard Keynes.

Keynes too was a practitioner as well as a theoretician. Long before Keynes wrote his masterwork, *The General Theory of Employment, Interest and Money*, he had worked as an economist for the British delegation at the Paris Peace Conference in 1919 following the end of the First World War. His experience in Paris and his dismay at what he saw as the ruinous terms of the peace treaty with defeated Germany prompted him to write a most remarkable book, *The Economic Consequences of the Peace*.[3] The book, translated into many languages, became a massive bestseller. It made the case that the harsh terms dictated to Germany by the victors would lead to the ruin of all of Europe. Writing passionately, he made the argument that Germany must be brought back into the fold of the European powers and that the idea of collecting enormous reparations from the Germans must be discarded. German prosperity, he argued, would enrich the British and French far more surely than would keeping Germany poor and dangerously resentful.

From this practical beginning, Keynes went on to assail the approach of the classical economists on how economies should be set on a successful course. He developed a model of the economy that showed that the equilibrium sought by classical economists could be achieved without an economy performing anywhere near its capacity. During the Great Depression of the 1930s, Keynes's critique of the classical model was devastatingly perceptive. According to Keynes, government needed to play a crucial role in jump-starting the economy during bad times. He showed that the approach of traditional governments in the face of high unemployment and slow growth was exactly wrong. Traditional governments cut expenditures when the economy slowed down and their revenues fell. In doing that, they added momentum to the downturn instead of countering it. Keynes reasoned that governments needed to play a counter-cyclical role. During periods of recession or depression governments should increase their spending, which would in turn result in a higher demand for goods and services, to which businesses would respond by increasing production and hiring more workers. Governments should also cut taxes and lower interest rates. Then, when the economy recovered and was operating at full throttle, governments should reverse these policies by reducing their spending, raising taxes, and increasing interest rates. Through these methods governments would lean against the prevailing direction of the economy—applying stimulus during slow times and stepping on the brakes when the economy was overheating. In this way governments could play an indispensable role in keeping the economy on an even keel.

What made Keynesian economics the preferred model, in one form or another, for postwar governments had at least as much to do with the political and societal alliances of the war and the postwar years as with the recognition that Keynes had hit upon ways of keeping countries from falling back into depression. The achievements of the golden decades rested on the foundation of a unique political alliance that had formed during the military and political struggle against the fascists and Nazis prior to and during the Second World War. Customarily the war has been understood in military terms, but the politics of the engagement was equally or even more crucial. By 1945 the alliance against Hitler's Germany extended politically from patriots on the right such as Churchill and Charles de Gaulle all the way to the Communists on the left, with liberals and social democrats somewhere in the middle.

The circuitous route by which the wartime grand alliance was achieved was only complete with the entrance of both the Soviet Union and the United States into the war in 1941. The most important political consequence of the alliance was the isolation, for a period of time—a relatively brief time as it turned out—of those on the far right of the political spectrum.

The victors of the Second World War included those who were determined to restructure society to establish full employment, higher living standards, and social benefits for working people. What happened was the outcome of contradictions and struggles within society that were much influenced by changing technology and the organization of the economy. Industrial workers emerged from the war better organized than ever in Britain, the United States, and Canada. In France, West Germany, and Italy, in the aftermath of Vichy, Nazism, and fascism, the thirst of workers for socialism was a great political force that had to be addressed.

In part, the acceptance by governments of responsibility for job creation was an outcome of the wartime economies in the United States, Canada, and Britain. Prior to the war, for the most part, politicians had told people that there was nothing governments could do to create jobs. Job creation was up to business, and all governments could do was to run a competent operation and keep public finances in order. But after the war broke out, governments transformed their role. They spent money as they had been unprepared to do before the conflict. They assumed responsibility for the overall performance of industry. Men and women who had been out of work for years quickly found jobs. In Canada, when the private sector was not in a position to meet industrial targets, the government created Crown corporations to get the job done. Private companies sent many of their best managers and executives to Ottawa to work for the government for the nominal sum of one dollar a year. The "dollar-a-year-men" played a key role in mobilizing the nation for wartime production in both the public and private sectors.

For populations who had learned first-hand that governments could plan their economies and achieve full employment, the idea of returning to the terrible days of unemployment and insecurity was unthinkable. In Canada the social-democratic Cooperative Commonwealth Federation (CCF), which had been on the margin of Canadian politics during the Depression, grew enormously in popular support during the war. In 1943 a Gallup Poll showed the CCF in first place among voters, just ahead of the governing Liberals. In 1944 Tommy Douglas led the CCF to an overwhelming victory in the provincial election in Saskatchewan. The CCF had been preaching economic planning by governments for years. Now Canadians were taking the party seriously. The burgeoning support for the CCF was one of the major reasons why the Liberal government of Mackenzie King undertook the creation of social programs and committed itself to overseeing job creation.

In addition to fiscal policies geared to achieving full employment, governments established social programs and opened the doors to higher education to a much wider segment of the population. In Canada and the United States, in the years immediately following the war, tens of thousands of veterans, funded by their national governments, enrolled in universities. These mature, experienced newcomers—mostly from working-class backgrounds—transformed the universities, changing them from the institutions for the privileged few that they had been in the past.

The social, economic, and political tide that sustained the advance of working people continued, with ups and downs, in Western Europe and North America until the end of the 1960s. By then the forces that had propelled the progressive advances of the golden decades were losing their ascendancy. For one thing, the political right had evolved a new set of doctrines that were to take it far in challenging the liberal ascendancy in both the United States and Britain.

The new conservative ideology of small government that represented an alternative to liberalism put in a first national appearance in the United States when Arizona Senator Barry Goldwater won the Republican Party's presidential nomination in 1964. By the early 1970s the thinking had advanced much further. From a number of disparate sources, a new conservatism was taking shape in the United States and in Britain. In the mid-1950s William F. Buckley Jr. had founded the *National Review*, a magazine around which conservatives of differing viewpoints could coalesce. Buckley's goal was to avoid divisive doctrinal questions, on issues such as civil rights, that might divide the right and to steer clear of the far-right extremists who identified with such fringe groups as the John Birch Society.

Long before Buckley launched the *National Review*, writers and thinkers who would become apostles in the lexicon of neo-conservatism were at work. In the 1940s F.A. Hayek, the godfather of neo-conservatism, began producing works that would serve as foundation stones of the new conservatism. As has been the case for Karl Marx, many of whose adherents found his works impenetrable, it is the idea of Hayek rather than the actual texts that has more often been inspirational to those in the new right. In influence Hayek was joined by Irving Kristol, and later writers such as Norman Podhoretz, the editor of *Commentary* magazine in New York. Podhoretz, like a number of other neo-conservative thinkers, began on the liberal side of the spectrum and later moved right, taking his magazine with him. Also of crucial importance to the vibrant new right was Milton Friedman, the University of Chicago economist who developed the monetarist school of economics long before it was to become fashionable as the leading alternative to Keynesianism in the 1970s.

———————

Just how did the world change to usher out one historical age and bring in another?

By the beginning of the 1970s, the global economic system, planned by the Americans in conjunction with their allies at Bretton Woods in 1944, was in distress. The Bretton Woods system was established on the faulty assumption that the United States would remain the unshakably dominant economic power into the indefinite future. Currency exchange rates were kept artificially low for the West German deutschmark and the Japanese yen vis-à-vis the dollar, which aided these countries in designing their postwar recoveries around export-oriented industries. Over time West German and Japanese industries in the automobile, machinery, and, later, electronics sectors became highly productive and posed potent threats to U.S. industry. Right from the start, the United States ran trade deficits with these countries. In effect, U.S. credit was being used to help build West Germany and Japan as bastions against the Soviet Empire.

By 1960 the perennial U.S. current account deficit vis-à-vis other countries was so great that all the gold held in the U.S. reserves, in places like Fort Knox, could not cover the value of the U.S. dollars held by foreign central banks. When a Yale economist first noticed this imbalance, the issue did not seem to have any practical implications. A decade later the situation had changed dramatically. By 1970 the United States had been waging a major war in Vietnam for the past six years. It was spending vast sums to fight the war at the same time as its industries were being squeezed by foreign competitors.

On August 15, 1971, the administration of President Richard Nixon took unilateral steps to stop the hemorrhaging of the U.S. economy. In a live television broadcast, Nixon announced that the United States was ending the link between the U.S. dollar and gold. The world's most powerful country eliminated the gold backing that foreign central banks assumed they had for the dollars they held. In addition, Nixon announced that the United States was establishing a temporary 10 per cent surcharge on imports into the country.

Finally, the Nixon administration established the Domestic International Sales Corporations (DISC), a tax scheme that enabled corporations to establish an entity through which they could conduct their exports. Under a company's DISC, exports were granted a rate of tax lower than the general rate. This was a straightforward export subsidy with the goal of enticing U.S. corporations to invest more in the United States and create jobs for Americans.

These U.S. initiatives were the beginning of the end of the Bretton Woods system. The Nixon administration proceeded to negotiate new exchange rates with its trading partners to lower the value of the dollar against their currencies so that the United States could correct its trade balance. The ultimate consequence of these initiatives was the collapse of fixed exchange rates in favour of a system of flexible exchange rates that exists to this day.

The onset of a rise in inflation and the demise of the Bretton Woods system were two elements in the new economic uncertainty that threatened the survival of the Keynesian system. A third element, and it was crucial, was the huge increase in the global price of petroleum that occurred in 1973–74. This event, exogenous to the

economic system itself, was a shock that pushed the global economy into a sharp recession accompanied by a fierce increase in
inflation. Between December 1973 and June 1974, the global price
of petroleum increased in two jumps from about $3 a barrel to
about $11 a barrel.

The consequence of these body blows to the economic system
was a prolonged period of economic stagnation in the industrialized world. It was the dreadful time of stagflation—the simultane-
ous existence of high inflation and high unemployment.

A look at the economic tables for all advanced countries, on
matters such as growth of Gross Domestic Product, rate of unemployment, inflation, and the onset of sustained government deficits,
reveals 1973 as a crucial turning point. Before 1973 the numbers
for all of these indicators tended to be benign. Growth was relatively strong, unemployment and inflation were relatively low, and
government deficits were modest. After 1973 the reverse was the
case. Growth slowed dramatically, unemployment and inflation
rose, and governments plunged into deficits to pay for their social
and educational programs.

These changes destroyed the fragile balances required to maintain Keynesianism. Higher and long-term joblessness reduced
government revenues at the same time as government outlays for
unemployment insurance and other forms of social assistance shot
upwards. In 1974 the governments in the advanced countries
plunged into deficit. As this happened, voices on the political right
began to insist that social programs were too expensive to sustain—
that the welfare state was a luxury that could not be afforded. No
sooner were long-term unemployment and a rise in the number
of people on welfare a reality than right-wing analysts made the
case that joblessness was the fault of those without work. The

unemployed lacked initiative. They didn't know how to adapt to changing patterns in the economy. Cases of welfare fraud or of people cheating on the system became major news stories, helping to spread the idea of a division between hard-working taxpayers and welfare bums who stayed home drinking beer and watching television. With long-term unemployment on the rise, the pool of jobless workers grew, undercutting the bargaining power of unions. The culture of solidarity that had underlain the golden decades was disintegrating. Conditions were ideal for a paradigm shift.

New business organizations were established to promulgate a tough conservative line to businessmen and the wider society. The U.S. Business Roundtable recruited CEOs of major companies into its ranks. Unlike the old Chambers of Commerce, the Roundtable had an alert, well-educated, young, and faithfully right-wing staff. The organization produced well-researched, accessible materials advocating policies for business and the country. The Roundtable acted as though it was a shadow cabinet, looking at the same issues as the president's cabinet and coming up with its own recommendations. The organization effectively lobbied Congress, the White House, and state legislators.

The Roundtable lobbied for tax cuts to restore profitability and competitiveness to business. It made the case that social programs and public funding of education had to be pared back. This line of thinking dovetailed with the work of social scientists who warned that social programs were reducing Americans to effete, dependent creatures who had lost the vibrant thirst for freedom. Authors such as Charles Murray, the Washington-based conservative theorist, spawned the concept of the "culture of dependency." While Murray's days of maximum influence did not arrive until the 1980s and 1990s, when he was taken very seriously in his advocacy of the repeal of federal welfare support for impoverished families (he supported the elimination of the federal program Aid for Families with Dependent Children, which was abolished in 1997), his attack on the welfare state was taking shape in the 1970s. In his mid-1980s book *Losing Ground* Murray listed the horrors he believed were the consequence of people living on welfare.⁴ Among the problems with welfare, according to Murray, was that it encouraged young women to have babies out of wedlock on the rational ground that this would make them eligible for federal welfare payments.

The writings of people like Murray illustrated how the narrative about social assistance was changing. Bolstering this line of thinking was an increasingly influential critique of the state that was to become one of the hallmarks of the new conservatism. While the large and active state has always been feared by those who favour laissez-faire capitalism, the state had also been understood by other conservatives as the embodiment of the nation, as the source of both domestic security and security from foreign enemies. In that version of conservative thought, the state was seen in positive terms.

What was new in the 1970s and later was the promulgation of the idea that the active state was inherently dangerous, that it could lead to the horrors of Nazi Germany and Stalinist Russia. In its less extreme forms, according to this line of thought, the state was bound to breed a noxious bureaucracy whose influence would be to lessen the creative power of business and of entrepreneurs.

As the forces of neo-conservatism coalesced in this period—while the ideas of their opponents were in disarray—a number of thinkers became privileged as inspirational and seminal to the new line of thought. One of them was Hayek, who developed a critique against the dangers of state control of the means of production. In his book *The Road to Serfdom* he argued that granting the state increasing control over the economy would lead not to a better life for people but to tyranny.[5]

By the mid-1970s a series of developments, a "perfect storm," if you like, converged to destroy the old paradigm on which the golden decades had been mounted and to bring a new paradigm to the centre of the economic and political stage.

One signal that a new age has succeeded an old one is that a novel set of ideas becomes dominant. The "ruling ideas" of what was to be the neo-liberal age differ markedly from the ideas that underlay the golden decades. During the neo-liberal age, the idea not just of a market economy but of a market society became entrenched. As a direct consequence, the idea of citizenship and the notion that there ought to be an essential equality among citizens were dethroned.

The economic doctrines that informed public policy during the neo-liberal age reinforced the power of employers against their employees. Monetarism rejected the idea that the state should directly promote full employment. Monetarism was a market-centred doctrine that held that the state was responsible for balancing its budgets and for ensuring the provision of an inflation-free money supply. The market would take care of the rest, efficiently allocating resources, incomes, and profits and determining the creation of employment. With this doctrine, economic theory returned to the fundamentals of mid-nineteenth-century classical liberalism. It became accepted that unemployment was natural to the market system and that efforts to achieve full employment would drive up costs and lead to high inflation and reduced returns on investment.

Monetarism was presented to the public as the economics of progress and freedom. The theory of monetarism contends that it is the responsibility of the central bank in a country to squeeze inflation out of the system by controlling the growth of the money supply. Advocates contend that inflation is like an addiction and that the sick nation that suffers from it needs to have its body-economic cleansed of it. At first the medicine is harsh, monetarists concede, but after that the patient recovers and goes on to lead a healthy life.

When monetarist medicine was applied by government the immediate consequences were harsh indeed for ordinary people as well as for many businesses. The world's first consciously applied monetarist experiment was carried out by the Thatcher government in Britain following the election of the Conservatives in 1979. Shrinking the money supply and making credit scarce to squeeze inflation out of the system had the effect of destroying a great number of jobs, driving up the unemployment rate and applying a hammer blow to the already ailing British manufacturing sector. The experiment was a success in the eyes of those who carried it out. Inflation fell rapidly. Much more to the point, for bondholders, who invested money, and for whom high inflation had cut sharply into their returns, the world was set on a better course. Indeed, the immediate effect of reduced inflation was a sharp real increase in the rate of return to bondholders.[6] What monetarism did in Thatcher's Britain was to secure the well-being of the crucial financial sector and the paramount position of the City of London.

The United States experimented with monetarism not long after Thatcher tried it in Britain. In November 1980, Ronald Reagan, the second of the great conservative leaders who changed the world, was elected president of the United States. The Reagan administration's experiment with monetarism was a rather muddied affair because while the monetarists were dominant in the ranks of the

U.S. right, a considerable number of advocates of supply-side economics also had influence. Supply-side economics—once described by George Bush Sr as "voodoo" economics—advocated tax cuts directed at corporations and high-income earners. The theory was that such tax cuts would so energize entrepreneurs and investors that they would produce new wealth and economic activity. The consequence of the new economic activity, according to the theory, would generate sufficient new tax revenues to make up for the tax cuts. The theory had some of the characteristics of a perpetual motion machine in the way it was supposed to generate new activities and new tax revenues.

Superficially, there is a resemblance between supply-side tax cuts and Keynesian tax cuts. Both act as a stimulus to the economy, but in quite different ways. Keynesian tax cuts are deliberately aimed at middle- and low-income earners because those are the people who have the highest propensity to consume. When low- or middle-income earners receive a tax cut, they are highly likely to spend the additional money on goods and services—which means that the stimulus pumped into the economy as a result of the spending carried out by these people is greater than is the case if the tax cut is directed at high-income people. When high-income people receive a tax cut, as they do in a supply-side program, they are much more likely to save it or invest it than are low- or middle-income earners. While stimulus is generated from such a tax cut, the gain is less than with a Keynesian tax cut. The process does, however, have the effect of increasing the government deficit, as is also the case with a Keynesian tax cut.

The Reagan administration's economic program involved three major elements: a sharp reduction in the growth of the money supply (the monetarist element implemented by the Federal Reserve

Board); a tax cut aimed at higher-income earners (the supply-side element); and a marked increase in military spending. The consequence was that the economy slowed dramatically in 1981 and then recovered, but the federal government deficit rose dramatically as did the U.S. trade and current account deficits. To call the administration's policy monetarism would be to simplify its overall thrust. Indeed, the negative consequences of Thatcher's monetarism were later offset by the expansionary thrust of the Reagan policies. As leading countries shifted to monetarism, they played a game that was known as "competitive deflation." While they cut back their government programs and tightened their monetary policies, they relied ever more on exporting goods to the United States, whose expansionary policies made the U.S. market crucial to all of them. Britain and the other European countries and Japan and Canada all achieved large trade surpluses with the United States. This configuration of commerce around the U.S. market was crucial in driving up the net indebtedness of the United States and putting the global economy on course to the crash of 2008.

In an article in the spring of 2009, Paul Krugman linked the crash of 2008 to the indebtedness that took off during the Reagan years:

It was the explosion of debt over the previous quarter-century [prior to 2008] that made the U.S. economy so vulnerable. Overstretched borrowers were bound to start defaulting in large numbers once the housing bubble burst and unemployment began to rise.

These defaults in turn wreaked havoc with a financial system that—also mainly thanks to Reagan-era deregulation—took on too much risk with too little capital.

There's plenty of blame to go around these days. But the prime villains behind the mess we're in were Reagan and his circle of advisers—men who forgot the lessons of America's last great financial crisis, and condemned the rest of us to repeat it.[7]

Monetarism fitted with the capitalist drive to find new sources of raw materials, and cheaper labour as well as markets outside the advanced countries. One of the fundamental weaknesses of the great social compromise of Keynesianism is that it rested on a balance of power between labour and capital that was unlikely to endure. During the postwar decades, in relation to what was to come later, and also in relation to the decades prior to the First World War, national economies were relatively self-contained. The era from the outbreak of the First World War in 1914 to the early 1970s was a lengthy period during which the rising globalization of the pre-1914 world came to an end. The 1920s boom, of course, was followed by the Great Depression of the 1930s and then by the Second World War. While the goal of the leading countries in the global system after 1945 was to expand trade, the movement of goods and services across frontiers, and especially the movement of capital from country to country, amounted to a mere fraction of what was to came later.

It was the relative autonomy of countries that made the major economic tools of Keynesianism viable. Increasing government spending and cutting taxes only worked to generate economic growth provided that almost all of the additional demand that was created was contained within the country itself. If the spurt of demand "leaked out" of the country, the experiment was spoiled. Indeed, it ended up being worse than useless, as was soon to become apparent after the mid-1970s.

Once trade boundaries came down and international commerce skyrocketed, the application of the Keynesian formula caused increased demand, but a growing portion of that demand took the form of purchases of goods and services from abroad. That leakage meant that many fewer jobs were created inside the country deploying the Keynesian policies. Such countries ended up with a rising external trade deficit, which had the additional effect of putting downward pressure on the value of their currencies vis-à-vis those of other countries.

Keynesianism, it turned out, was applicable only at a particular moment in the history of capitalism when the balance of power between labour and capital that existed at the end of the war was in place. Once business could seek labour and resources in the Third World on an enormous scale, this balance was overturned.

From the middle of the 1970s on, the trade patterns of the advanced countries altered dramatically. Up until that point most trade was conducted among the major countries, whose labour costs were comparable. After that date, imports from developing countries, where wages were dramatically lower, increased enormously. Corporations were shifting their quest for primary products to developing countries. In addition, manufacturers were establishing assembly plants in low-wage countries. Once it became possible for companies to shift production, in auto plants, for example, from the developed countries to low-wage countries, the ability of labour to bargain in the advanced countries was dealt a heavy blow.

In lockstep with monetarism came the concerted drive to privatize state-owned industries, telecommunications companies, railways, airlines, energy utilities, and water companies. It now became accepted as matter of faith—not supported by empirical evidence—that private companies were more efficient than companies owned

and operated in the public sector. Privatization typically underval-
ued public assets and ended up transferring vast wealth to private
owners, with the most extreme cases of this phenomenon occurring
in the former Soviet Union and Eastern Europe. The advanced
countries also carried through massive privatizations of state-
owned companies.

Successive waves of deregulation did away with the rules governing financial institutions, minimizing the distinctions among
deposit banking, investment banking, and insurance. This was when
the investment instruments—all manner of derivatives and futures
options—were legitimated to allow the lending of ever larger
amounts of capital, backed by ever smaller reserves of real assets.
The pyramid constructed was a self-propelling, self-consuming
pyre that could only survive through the continuous addition of
new debt, its essential fuel.

With the United States, and America's offshore island, the
United Kingdom, at the centre of the global system, the debt took
many forms. The old lesson, learned nearly three centuries ago
with the South Sea Bubble, is that bubbles are bound to burst, that
all the hype that attends their expansion is blown away in the cata-
clysmic instant when it all flies apart.

The era that ended with the crash of 2008 prized finance,
wealth, showy consumption, the acquisition of grand houses, private schools for the children of the privileged, and safaris to see
the Big Cats of Africa. Workers, craftsmen, teachers, farmers,
and nurses were not much valued. The affections of the era were
erratic, transitory, and rootless.

A central myth of the age was that a borderless world was in the
making. This was true enough for capital, but for labour, refugees,
and the wretchedly impoverished, it was a hard world in which

migrations to better places grew ever more perilous. Globalized economic production drove the poor off the land and into gigantic cities notable for their dreadful housing, sewage, and infrastructures. One milestone in this miserable era was that towards its end more than half of humanity had come to dwell in cities.

Particularly in the United States and the United Kingdom, but also in Canada, the whole idea of economic planning was disparaged as a fossilized relic from the bygone days of the mixed economy. The short term was what mattered. The long term could take care of itself. A major consequence of this mentality was the deterioration of public infrastructure. Highways, roads, bridges, rail systems, schools, universities, and hospitals were allowed to decline into ever greater states of dilapidation. An emblem of the public squalor of the age was the London Underground, the grand old lady of the world's rail subway systems. Journeys on the London Tube customarily began with passengers hearing the announcement of a long list of the lines or sections of lines that were, or soon would be, out of operation, or undergoing repairs.

The private opulence of the few was thought too important for it to be scaled back to provide resources to address the public squalor endured by the many. Catastrophes punctuated this reality. In 2005, when Hurricane Katrina ravaged New Orleans, not only were the levees a shambles, but there was also no plan to ensure that the poor, mostly black, residents who did not own cars could escape from the city. In 2007 thirteen people died when a highway bridge collapsed in Minnesota.

During the age that has ended, the hegemonic myth had it that the market, conceived as a natural, impersonal actor, set the monetary rewards for work according to the true worth of those doing the work. A top banker earned many millions of dollars a year in salary, bonuses, and stock options—and was considered to be worth that money because he could command it in the marketplace. Any interference with this magisterial process, through higher taxes or by regulating the amount of income that an individual could earn, would inexorably result in a loss of productivity that would not only damage the performance of the bank for which he worked, but also, by extension, retard the forward thrust of the economy and, therefore, the general well-being. It was a time when the dominant myth held that the real work was done in the office towers of financiers and corporate law firms, rather than in factories, fields, schools, laboratories, and hospitals, and on construction sites.

The neo-liberal order was the culmination of American-style capitalism worldwide. But neo-liberalism contained within it the seeds of its own destruction. The era in which it was entrenched turned out to be a sunset era, during which the United States' domination of the world began inexorably to decline.

The claim that the United States is a declining power in the global system has been made before. Each time the claim has been made, the Americans have apparently proven the naysayers wrong and have come back to resume their dominance. The first time the case was seriously made was in the mid-1970s, following the fall of Saigon and the collapse of Nixon's presidency after Watergate. A few years later neo-conservatives joined the ranks of the declinists, for the moment at least, when they argued that the Soviet Union had surpassed the United States as a military power. (A decade later, when the Soviet Empire and then the Soviet Union itself disintegrated, it became abundantly evident that the Soviet military, along with Soviet industry, was in an advanced state of decay, and that the earlier claim of Soviet military supremacy had been utterly bogus.) The next serious wave of declinist thinking arose in the 1980s, when Japanese industry and finance challenged U.S. industrial and financial leadership. The bursting of the Japanese real estate bubble, with its severe consequences for Japanese financial institutions, along with the great success of the tech-centred U.S. economy in the 1990s, made the theorists of decline look foolish once again.

Now the idea that the United States and its global system are in decline is in the air once more. The bursting of the tech stock bubble in the United States, the wars in Afghanistan and Iraq, and the crash of 2008 have raised urgent new questions about the ability of the United States to remain globally dominant. This time the perceived challenger is China, or Asia more generally.

Some critics may be inclined to discount the persistent and recurring theme of U.S. decline as little more than the fashionable pessimism of a civilization that has long been enamoured of investigations of its own demise. The idea that the West is in decline has been around for well over a century, and can be dismissed as little more than a cultural artifact. On the other hand, beginning in the mid-nineteenth century, serious analysts made the case, in recurrent waves, that the British Empire faced decline. While these analysts were not right at first, they and their successors were on the right track in pointing out the weaknesses of the British Empire and the advantages of its potential challengers.

When we review the cases made over the decades about U.S. decline, the major themes that have emerged have clearly been serious. In the 1970s the focus was on the U.S. inability to win a land war in Asia since the Second World War, on the stalemate in Korea and defeat in Vietnam. In the 1980s the discussion shifted to the emerging fiscal crisis in the United States, the country's descent into net indebtedness after enjoying a net surplus vis-à-vis the rest of the world since the end of the First World War. In addition, fingers pointed to the rise of Japanese industrial and financial prowess. The 1990s was the decade of reprieve for the United States, with the tech sector burgeoning, the concept of the "new economy" in the air, and both Japan and Europe in the doldrums.

Then came the dot.com crash in 2000, the wars, and the crash of 2008. The developments of the past decade, taken together with the rise of China and India, and the shift of global economic output ever more towards Asia, support a more general case for the decline of the United States. Indeed, the case was being made before the financial meltdown.

In his book *The Grand Chessboard* (1997), Zbigniew Brzezinski, who served as national security advisor during the presidency of Jimmy Carter from 1977 to 1981, argued that the unique position of the United States as a non-Eurasian power, able to dominate Eurasia, and therefore, the world, was certain to decline. "Since America's unprecedented power is bound to diminish over time," he asserted, "the priority must be to manage the rise of other regional powers in ways that do not threaten America's global primacy."[8]

In my book *The Perils of Empire: America and Its Imperial Predecessors* (2008), I argued that the United States was an empire that was overstretched militarily and economically, and that the country faced the prospect of playing a substantially reduced role in the future in the global system of power. On the broader question of the geostrategic position of the United States, I stated: "Everywhere one looks, the United States faces a series of interrelated problems. While the American Empire is by no means in imminent peril of collapse, it could be forced to pull back from some of its more exposed positions in the world trouble spots, in particular the Middle East."[9]

With respect to the economy, I made this case:

In the near future, the excesses of American economic policy are bound to force a painful period of adaptation and restructuring. The accumulated debt to foreigners, the current account deficit, and Washington's budget deficit will all have to be faced, either through a protracted period of adjustment, the famed "soft landing," or through a hard landing that necessitates rapid adaptation. Such a hard landing could occur as the result of a major recession caused by a spike in oil prices to the range of one hundred dollars a barrel, the bursting of the property price bubble (long overdue in both the United States and the United Kingdom), or a U.S. military showdown with Iran. These adjustments, when they come, are virtually guaranteed to force radical changes in the economic relationship of both the United States and the UK (which has pursued a similar economic strategy) with the rest of the world. The sky-high trade surpluses of China and, to a lesser extent of Japan, will have to be corrected and scaled back. These developments will generate two further effects worth noting: the end of China's wide-open market in the United States, which will necessitate serious adjustments to Chinese economic policy, and pressure on the United States (and the UK) to ramp up the goods-producing sectors of their economies.

What is coming is no less than the dethroning of the United States as the central economy around which the global system revolves. The First World War had similar consequences for the British, who felt the pain of adjustment for decades afterward. At the end of the great cycle of changes to come, neither of the major English-speaking countries will be positioned at the apex of the global economy. This is not to predict that the United States will have an unimportant economic role to play or will cease to be productive. On the other hand, they will no longer enjoy the extra benefits that have gone with presiding over the world's central economy. As debtors, Americans will be pushed down the ladder of the world division of labor in favor of the world's more financially sound creditor economies, likely the Japanese, Europeans, and Chinese, among others.[10]

The reason for including this rather lengthy quote from my book, which was published in spring 2008, before the crash occurred, is that I believe analysts should be held to account for the predictions they make.

Now that the once revered supermen of the age have flown the economy into the side of a mountain, the wreckage lies all around us. The myths of the supermen have been exposed as the fabrications of con men who enriched themselves at the expense of humanity. The price that will now be paid by people the world over for the rule of the financiers will be stupendous. One thing people everywhere have gained, though, is freedom from the power of the lies that they were told. And that freedom can be the basis for a new beginning.

Chapter Nine

THE COMING GLOBAL ECONOMY

———————

AFTER THE CRASH the next global economy will centre less on
the United States and much more on Asia, and more important
roles will be played in it by Europe and Latin America. The proportion of global economic output accounted for by the United
States has been declining for over sixty years, from about 50 per
cent after the Second World War to about 20 per cent today. As the
U.S. share of global output drops to the range of 15 per cent, qualita-
tive changes in the role of the United States in the world will make
themselves felt.

Even though the U.S. proportion of global output has steadily
fallen, the United States has until now retained its crucial economic leverage. The 20 per cent share that the United States held
up until the crash remained the critical 20 per cent, and the United
States retained its position at the centre of the global system in its
ability to determine outcomes to a much greater extent than any
other economic power. For crucial rising economic powers, most
notably China, the U.S. market was essential to increasing economic
output and economic development at home. But this condition is

changing—and this is a change that will be of great importance for the new global economy.

For the past six decades, an essential aspect of the U.S. role as the global economic hegemonic power has been to open its domestic market as the market of last resort to most of the countries of the world. As well, the United States has served as the site of last resort for investments from other countries. Americans have been the world's crucial spenders, and they have accommodated the world's savers. All of this has been enormously beneficial, of course, to Americans, who have in general been enabled to live beyond their means.

In the long term China appears to be the country that could ultimately stand to gain the most from the changes that are coming to the global economy. In the short to middle term, however, China's way of dealing with the rest of the world is being subjected to a wrenching transformation.

For China, the pattern of trade and capital flows with the United States will be fundamentally altered. In recent years China has been running up enormous trade surpluses with the United States. Had China allowed the exchange rate of the yuan to float against other currencies, principally the U.S. dollar, the surpluses would have driven up the value of the yuan, which would have braked the further rise of the exports. Instead China decided to keep the yuan and the dollar closely aligned. To prevent the yuan from soaring against the dollar, China had to allow dollars to flood in so that the Chinese accumulated an ever more enormous cache of dollars. That was how China ended up as the holder of in excess of U.S.$1 trillion in U.S. treasury bills, bonds with a very low rate of return.

In the early months of 2009, as the implications of the crash and the nature of the coming global economy began to dawn on people everywhere, as Paul Krugman wrote, "China's leaders woke up and realized that they had a problem." China, like many other countries, was recognizing, as Krugman said, that it was saddled with an "excess of dollars." The rules of the game, Krugman reported, had "changed in a fundamental way," but China's leaders had not yet come to grips with that fact. "Two years ago, we lived in a world in which China could save much more than it invested and dispose of the excess savings in America. That world is gone." China would have to face up to the new and difficult challenges of the global crisis—as would the Japanese, the Europeans, and, Krugman advised, the Americans as well.[1]

Chinese society itself has begun to deeply experience the effects of a changing relationship with the United States. According to official Chinese statistics, China has a vast pool of migrant workers, totalling some 130 million people, who leave their homes, often in rural regions, to travel to the giant metropolises to find work. As a consequence of the economic crash, in particular the severe slump in Chinese exports, about twenty million of these migrant workers had lost their jobs by the winter of 2009. Chen Xiwen, director of the office that advises China's ruling Communist Party on policies affecting farmers, reported that roughly 15 per cent of the migrant workers were without work in late January. Thousands of factories had closed because of the declining export market. Chen warned that with six million new migrant labourers entering the job market each year, as the newcomers seek employment they will be competing with the twenty million who are now out of work. He acknowledged that unemployed rural migrant workers have held mass demonstrations in various regions of the country.[2]

China has been thrown into a very real economic crisis as a consequence of the financial meltdown and recession in the United States. The Chinese state has awesome problems that it must face. With a population more than twice the size of the European Union, and a continuum of social conditions ranging from the wealthiest to the poorest that makes the divisions between, say, Rumania and Germany appear to be minor, China is negotiating one of the greatest economic transformations in human history. Between three and four hundred million people have incomes and living standards considerable higher than the level of the poor peasantry that constitutes the majority of China's population.

The leadership of the Communist Party is acutely aware that presiding over a society divided into so many disparate elements—from the highly educated professionals and members of the business class to those who eke out a bare living on the land—is fraught with the risk of political upheaval, even social revolution. Those directing the Chinese state have devised a system of state capitalism that allows for buccaneer-style capitalism in leading sectors of the economy along with a planning apparatus that feeds migrant workers into the workplace and uses the incomes they earn to help lift the peasantry out of poverty. The availability of the vast U.S. market for Chinese exports has been central to the operation of this system. Chinese capitalists and the Chinese state found it more profitable and more manageable to use the U.S. market to pull themselves up by their bootstraps than to make the more difficult choice of developing their own vast internal market. In following the path to industrialization by holding down the value of its currency and emphasizing exports to the United States, China was following in the footsteps of West Germany and Japan, countries that took the same course with great success during the postwar decades.

In 2007, according to World Bank figures, China's exports were valued at $1.22 trillion, about 37 per cent of the country's GDP. About 58 per cent of these exports were made up of products designed elsewhere; parts and components were imported into China for assembly of the end product, which was then exported. This is the trade pattern of an industrializing country, which relies heavily on outside technology and research and development. (It also resembles the pattern of Canada's manufacturing exports, for that matter, which illustrates the failure of Canada to develop beyond this stage of industrialization.) A vast amount of imports go into the making of Chinese exports. Taking these imports into account, the weight of Chinese exports as a proportion of GDP is more realistically about 12 per cent—still enormous, but much less overwhelming than suggested by the 37 per cent figure.

On the eve of the crash, China's exports were growing at a pace of 25 per cent annually, more than twice the rate of growth of China's GDP—a figure that indicates the importance of exports as the leading edge of China's growth. The figure also points to the unsustainable nature of the Chinese trade pattern even prior to the crash. If China's exports had continued to grow at this rapid pace, by 2020 50 per cent of the world's exports would be accounted for by this one country, compared with 10 per cent today. That is simply not possible, either economically or geopolitically. For one thing, China's economic development over the past couple of decades has significantly pushed up the cost of Chinese labour, which has already been pushing exporters to switch their production to lower-cost countries such as India and Vietnam. The profile of Chinese trade was bound to alter, and the economic crisis is speeding that change along.

While the U.S. market for Chinese products is bound to be less bountiful than in the past, other markets can partially fill the void.

The European market is probably going to be one of them. The greatest potential, however, lies with India, the other Asian giant that is swiftly becoming a global economic power. Commercial relations between China and India have grown enormously, and will continue to grow over the coming decades. The fit between the giants is one in which China plays the role of industrial producer to India's role as a high-tech powerhouse. Recently China has increased its exports to India in sectors such as capital goods, including power plants and other infrastructure equipment. With these exports, rather than relying on products designed elsewhere, as is the case for most of the Chinese exports to the United States, the Chinese designed and developed the capital goods sold to India and retained much of the value added from these sales.[3]

Over the next couple of decades, trade within Asia, the continent with 60 per cent of the world's population, will come to dominate global trade. In addition to trade between India and China, there has already been an enormous increase in trade between China and Japan; and if we include Russia (a country with territory in both Europe and Asia), trade within Asia will grow even more significant as a proportion of the global total. Russia is certain to play a key role in selling petroleum to the other great Asian powers.

Despite the opportunity for very large trade relationships with Asian powers and countries in other parts of the world, the role of trade in Chinese growth is going to diminish. China is being forced to turn to the enormous task of developing the internal market. Over the long term the turn to the domestic market will cement China's position as the world's leading economic power. Over the medium term the transition will provoke huge strains within Chinese society. So far the return of millions of former Chinese factory workers to rural villages, where they work for much less pay as farm labourers than they had become accustomed to, has been managed without major societal or political upheaval. The rural villages may serve as a safety net as China passes through its difficult transition. Yet political protest on a scale that makes it hard to ignore could erupt from the villages among the laid-off factory workers.

China is going through the process of becoming a mature economy in which the whole of the Chinese population will share in the country's economic output to a much greater extent than today. As this occurs, exports will decline as a proportion of China's GDP. Indeed, China will become a much greater importer, particularly of commodities from many regions of the world, including Canada.

The United States will pass through its own wrenchingly difficult transition in which it becomes only one of the major global economic powers rather than the paramount one. En route the United States will lose the privileges it enjoyed as the world's supreme power, its ability to run a multi-decade-long current account deficit, to become indebted to the rest of the world on a long-term basis, and to have its dollar serve as the world's reserve currency. As a consequence, the perks that Americans enjoyed as they accumulated their vast indebtedness to the rest of the world will now become charges against them as they pay it down. With that long journey out of indebtedness will go a falling standard of living for the average American. Still, this "end of empire" odyssey will bring new economic opportunities to enrich those clever enough to climb onboard. One of these possibilities will come in the launching of manufacturing operations in the United States as U.S. labour costs fall relative to those in other parts of the world that have rising labour costs. As a great continental nation, with an immense population, the descent out of world-empire status can be more graceful in the United States than it was in the case of the United Kingdom, a small island off the coast of Europe that was reduced to minor-league status when its imperial possessions declared their independence.

As the global economy shifts away from the U.S.-centred system of the decades following the end of the Second World War, a new hegemonic power on the same scale is unlikely to emerge for at least the next three or four decades. Instead, we will live in a multipolar world with a global economy dominated by a number of leading powers. This list will surely include the United States, European Union, China, Japan, India, Russia, Brazil, and Nigeria. No single state will have the power to enforce a common set of rules and norms within the system. While the existence of multinational corporations and the regulatory authority of the World Trade Organization will counter the shift to a world with multiple centres of power and ways of doing things, these institutions will not halt that shift. No single system along the lines of the neo-liberal system of recent decades will be in place everywhere. The consequence of this is that super-regions under the domination of one or several of the leading states could well emerge.

For a variety of reasons, the new economy will be less global, at least over the middle-range future, than it was during the years leading up to the crash of 2008. The United States will no longer serve as the singular focus of global consumption and finance. Peak oil, in combination with the rising price of oil over the long-term, will add considerably to the costs of shipping basic manufactured products, food, and raw materials over long distances. The days in which China is responsible for an outsized proportion of the manufacturing for North Americans and Europeans are drawing to an end.

PART TWO

The Crash in Canada

Chapter Ten

CANADA'S POLITICAL

RESPONSE TO THE CRASH:

AN EXERCISE IN DENIAL

_____

CANADA'S POLITICAL LEADERS were slow to acknowledge the very existence of an economic crisis. During the federal election campaign that culminated in the election of a new Parliament on October 14, 2008, the leaders of the country's political parties steadfastly ignored the collapse of financial institutions in the United States and Europe and the crash of the world's stock markets, including those in Canada. During the last two weeks of the campaign, with global markets in free fall, the leaders plodded on, offering up programs that had little relevance in light of the frightening realities that had overtaken them.

Stephen Harper, the prime minister who had called the election in violation of his own government's law fixing dates for federal elections, had hoped to cruise to a majority victory against Liberal leader Stéphane Dion, who been effectively branded by Conservative advertising and the compliant national media as hapless, ineffectual, and unfit for office. Harper and his finance minister, Jim Flaherty, insisted during the campaign that all was well in Canada and that, under no circumstances, would the government of Canada be forced to run a deficit. As the alarums offstage of a global economic crisis grew ever louder, the Conservatives blithely claimed that to the extent that there was a problem their government had anticipated it months earlier with tax cuts that would provide the country with whatever economic stimulus it required. Canada's financial institutions were sound, Harper and Flaherty insisted. Canada's economy was the envy of the world, well suited to making the country an island of well-being during the rising global storm.

Dion's Liberals were equally unresponsive to the onset of the economic crisis. They merely warned that the Conservative government's tax cuts had imprudently removed the fiscal cushion that was Canada's guarantee against a descent into deficits. The Liberals, Dion insisted, were sound economic managers. Their programs had been costed, were affordable, and could be implemented without deficit-spending. The Liberals presented themselves as the golden mean of Canadian politics, unlike the Conservatives, whose tax-cutting agenda was fiscally irresponsible, and the New Democrats, who would have to use "Monopoly money" to fund their promises.

The New Democrats—led by Jack Layton, who announced that he was presenting himself to the electorate as a serious choice for prime minister—also claimed that their program could be implemented while keeping the federal government's budget in balance.

The parties remained locked in a political struggle whose narrative had been cast in stone before the election was called at a time when the nation's leaders showed not the slightest awareness that a momentous crisis in the global economy had already begun.

Canada's political parties, their leaders, and the mainstream media that covered them were living in their own special world that was remote from reality in the autumn of 2008. Canada would soon pay a very heavy price for the complacency of those at the helm.

For the first few weeks following the federal election on October 14, 2008, the Conservatives continued to insist that the government would not be required to run a deficit. For their part, the Liberals charged that the government's poor fiscal management was going to return Ottawa to a deficit following a long string of Liberal government surpluses. With financial institutions and stock markets crashing, the consensus among economic analysts in many countries was that the world was facing the most severe economic crisis since the Great Depression. The partisan debate between Canada's two largest parties, conducted on assumptions that were thoroughly out of date, contributed to the torpid Canadian response to the crisis.

Finance Minister Flaherty showed no more understanding of the crash than did the prime minister. On October 23, after the federal election was safely over and the economic crisis was making headlines daily all over the world, Flaherty boasted about the state of the economy:

> Our economic fundamentals are the strongest in the G7. I'm proud to serve as the Finance Minister and travel abroad and meet with my G7 colleagues. I was speaking with one of them this morning on the phone in Europe. Our economic fundamentals are the envy of the G7. We run balanced budgets here. . . . As I say, other nations are envious of our situation.

Towards the end of his speech he added:

Let me conclude by repeating that our economy has solid economic fundamentals, and Canadians can take some pride in that. I can assure you that our budget will remain balanced. We do have the strongest economic fundamentals in the G7. I can also assure you that our spending will be controlled.

Let me end with three good reasons to be optimistic about Canada and our economy. Our economy is strong. Our government is focused with strong leadership by Prime Minister Stephen Harper. And our country is united. My friends, we have a brilliant future together and I thank you for the invitation to be with you today.[1]

In their conviction that Canada has no fundamental economic interests apart from those of the United States, the members of the Harper government have obstinately manifested the Canadian tendency to cling to forms of economic dependency that are profoundly at odds with the interests of Canadians. The case of Flaherty is instructive. Many have made the argument that for a finance minister to insist that Canada would not run a deficit only six months before he had to announce that there would be a $50 billion deficit is evidence of his staggering incompetence. That may be, but more to the point, it reveals the extent to which he is a true believer in the precepts of neo-liberalism and in the wholesome economic effects of the U.S. connection for Canada. More than being unwilling to share the truth with Canadians about what was coming, Flaherty and Harper could not fathom what was coming. The pillars of their world were collapsing all around them.

While Canadian political leaders were playing the game of "See No Evil" during the election campaign, much more penetrating debates were taking place in the United States and United

Kingdom. Barack Obama, as the Democratic Party's nominee for the presidency, was using the election campaign to bring home the economic disaster to the American people. In Britain, Prime Minister Gordon Brown, the leader of the Labour Party, had been falling in the polls and seemed unable to ignite any enthusiasm for his leadership among the British people. But he seized the failing economy as his issue and showed that he understood what the stakes were in the financial collapse.

Canada's slower descent into recession (compared with the United States) and the absence of the collapse of financial institutions and a foreclosure crisis induced a mood of considerable complacency in the Conservative government and in the national media. The tone altered with the sudden onset of a political furor that threatened the survival of the Harper government in late November 2008. Having called Parliament into session for the first time since the election, and having unveiled its Speech from the Throne, the government presented a financial statement, unleashing a storm. Flaherty's financial statement was inept as a summary of the economy's true state. Politically, it was a colossal blunder. By the time Flaherty delivered a document that was both long on self-congratulation because Canadian banks had not collapsed and short on acumen about what the crisis portended for Canada, the world was in a different space than it had been six weeks earlier when Canadians cast their ballots in a general election.

For one thing, the severity of the global economic crisis had become glaringly apparent. For another, on November 4, Obama had won the presidency of the United States in a commanding victory that reconfigured the electoral map of that country. His triumph ended four decades during which the Republican Party, with its Southern strategy and its backlash racial agenda, had made the GOP the country's "natural governing party." As president-elect, Obama faced the reality of the economic crisis head-on. That fact, and Flaherty's ill-judged inclusion of a scheme to sharply reduce the public funding on which Canada's political parties relied, brought the opposition parties to life.

Behind the scenes, Liberal, NDP, and Bloc Québécois insiders negotiated a political compact designed to defeat the Harper government and bring to office a Liberal-NDP coalition government. To ensure the parliamentary majority that the proposed government would require, the BQ undertook not to make a vote of non-confidence in the proposed coalition government for at least eighteen months. Under the arrangement, the NDP would hold one-quarter of the seats in the cabinet, not to include the Ministry of Finance. The 162 members of parliament from the three parties signed an undertaking to vote down the Conservative government and to replace it with the new government. That signed statement notified the Governor General that the majority of members of the House of Commons had lost confidence in the present government and were prepared to bestow their confidence on the proposed Liberal-NDP ministry.

Faced with the near certainty of the fall of his government, Harper seized on a means of retaining power that was constitutionally novel and raised troubling questions about the future of parliamentary democracy in Canada. He sought from the Governor General the prorogation of the session of parliament that had just begun. His motive was entirely transparent. It was to prevent the defeat in the House of Commons of his government's economic statement, a confidence motion that would have brought down the government. Never before had a prime minister requested prorogation—a device used to punctuate the achievements of Parliament over a lengthy period of time and to refocus the government with a new session and a new Speech from the Throne—solely to avoid defeat. Perhaps foolishly, on December 4 Governor General Michaëlle Jean agreed to the prorogation.

Without doubt, the decision will require careful thinking in the future to close the loophole Harper found to extend the life of a government that had lost the legitimacy that flowed from the support of the majority of the members of Parliament.

In December–January, with Parliament no longer in session, events moved swiftly. Dion had been abruptly dumped as Liberal leader in a virtual palace coup in the party. The Liberals altered their method for choosing a new leader, and the party's parliamentary caucus selected Michael Ignatieff as interim leader, with the official selection to be confirmed later, at a party convention to be held in May 2009. (And at that party convention, held in Vancouver, Ignatieff was duly endorsed as leader.) The Harper government, long a proponent of an elected Senate, chose this hiatus to install eighteen new Senators, the largest number ever appointed at one time.

The decisive hurdle on which the life of the government would depend when parliament resumed sitting in late January 2009 would be to win the passage of its budget. Interim Liberal leader Ignatieff, who had made his coolness to the idea of a Liberal-NDP coalition government clear from the outset, held the fate of the Harper government in his hands when Flaherty presented the budget on January 27.

In one way the Conservative government's budget transformed the rhetoric about the state of the economy and the fiscal position of the federal government. Only a couple of months earlier Harper and Flaherty were still shrugging off the very suggestion that Ottawa would need to run a deficit. Flaherty's budget declared that the federal government deficit would total $64 billion over the next two years. Much of that projected deficit was accounted for by the impact of the tax cuts that the Harper government had made before the economic crisis took hold with a vengeance. Some of the rest came as a consequence of proposed new tax cuts. The budget included across-the-board income tax cuts that not only benefited lower-income earners but all income earners. Although the finance minister presented the tax cuts as measures to stimulate the economy, they were unlikely to have much effect in lifting the economy. A sizeable portion of the cuts would go to paying down existing debts or replenishing lost savings. A further and very large chunk would be spent on imported goods. Canadians import over $400 billion worth of goods a year, close to 30 per cent of our GDP. By way of contrast, Americans import goods equivalent to about 15 per cent of their GDP. A huge portion of the tax cuts announced by Flaherty were bound to leak out of Canada in the purchase of additional imports. They might stimulate the Chinese, Japanese, and U.S. economies, but they would do precious little to stimulate the Canadian economy.

When we cut through all the details in the budget, one central fact emerges. The amount of money the government planned to spend directly to stimulate the economy was far too low to save jobs and to mitigate the effects of the recession on Canadians and their communities.

Depending on how you interpret the budget, the government committed itself to direct new spending of about $10 billion to $12 billion on infrastructure and housing over a two-year period. Some of this depended on matching provincial and municipal funds, which might never materialize. Much of it depended on how much the government would actually spend, a crucial matter because the

Harper government has left most of the previous infrastructure money it promised in earlier budgets unspent. Indeed, in an early June 2009 meeting in Whistler, B.C., the mayors of the country's twenty-two largest cities complained that the annual construction season was well underway and their cities had received precious little of the economic stimulus promised by the federal government in its budget. Toronto Mayor David Miller told the media, "Although there've been announcements, very little money has hit the ground." Carl Zehr, the mayor of Kitchener, Ontario, and chairman of the big-city mayors caucus, complained, "This construction season is virtually lost." The mayors of the biggest cities warned that the country's municipalities faced a $123 billion "infrastructure deficit" and that the stimulus spending was much needed.[2]

At most, the new direct spending announced in the budget by the Harper government amounted to about $6 billion a year.

This number may sound big. In fact, it is puny. The Canadian Gross Domestic Product totals about $1.5 trillion a year. The $6 billion a year amounts to just over one-half of 1 per cent of Canada's GDP. Economic announcements and forecasts told Canadians that the country was on track to lose hundreds of thousands of jobs during the months following the presentation of the budget. The Conservative government's planned spending would create, at most, about sixty thousand short-term jobs.

The critical political question was how Ignatieff, the new Liberal leader, would respond to the budget. He delayed his response for twenty-four hours. His decision, when it came, was as momentous as was the announcement not many weeks before that the Liberals and the NDP planned to form a coalition government with the support of the Bloc Québécois. At his press conference at the National Press Theatre in Ottawa, Ignatieff announced that the

Liberals would support the budget provided that the Conservatives agreed to the passage of an amendment to it requiring the government to provide periodic updates on how the budget is working.

Explaining himself in answer to questions from the media, the Liberal leader was embarrassingly sophomoric. The Liberal-NDP coalition had been useful, he said, because it had forced the government to put many useful measures in the budget. On the other hand, he said the budget remained a "Conservative" budget that would probably not work. Nonetheless, he said he intended to vote for it. Provided, of course, that his amendment was acceptable to Harper. By turns, Ignatieff sounded like Demosthenes, thundering down condemnation on a government that has repeatedly failed Canadians and then like an apple-polishing pupil asking for a report card from the head master. During his news conference, he announced sonorously that the Liberals would watch the Conservatives "like hawks."

As a consequence of the decision to support the Flaherty budget, Ignatieff tore up the proposed Liberal-NDP coalition agreement and aligned himself with the Conservatives on the fundamentals of economic policy. Before the Conservatives introduced the budget, the Liberal leader had insisted that the budget belonged to the Conservatives, not to his party. Having opted to vote for it, however, and having destroyed the coalition alternative, Ignatieff made the Flaherty budget his own. In addition to demolishing the coalition, the Liberal leader disarmed the one opposition weapon that the Harper government most feared—the ability to vote the government down and to replace it without forcing a new election on the country. Having used their votes to pass the budget, the Liberals made the government viable, making it a virtual certainty that any time Harper wanted an election, he could go to the

Governor General and obtain the dissolution of the House, or he could engineer his government's defeat in parliament on a vote of confidence.

As the deadly effects of the economic crisis took hold in the loss of tens of thousands of jobs, as families coped with the anxiety of making ends meet, as hard-hit communities such as Windsor, Ontario, struggled to sustain a viable future, serious politics at the federal level disappeared the moment that Ignatieff made his fateful choice.

A few days after the Liberals decided to support the Harper government's budget, the horror of the economic crisis hit home as it had not before with the release of Canada's unemployment statistics for January 2009. The Canadian figures were worse than those in the United States. Canada lost 129,000 jobs, compared to 598,000 jobs lost south of the border. Ontario was hit with the loss of another 71,000 jobs.[3] The manufacturing sector was not simply being hit. It was being demolished.

When confronted with the numbers, Liberal MPs rose during Question Period to demand that the government do more. Harper did not take the Liberal questions seriously. He said, "We cannot have in Parliament, quite frankly, instability every week and every month, every time there's a new number, people demanding a different plan."[4]

Ignatieff, the self-designated Hawk, had momentarily had his chance and let it slip away. Harper was back in charge, and the prime minister knew it. Harper faced down the Hawk when the threat was serious. He was not likely to be stampeded by the sight of his feathered foe the next time.

———————

Having spent a couple of weeks in the United States in March 2009, when the fury against the bonuses for AIG executives was at its height, I could not believe the difference in tone when I got back to Canada. There was plenty of anger among those losing jobs in Canada, but once Ignatieff killed the Liberal-NDP coalition and lined up with Harper on the budget, the lid was clamped on. In Canada the anger was subterranean, more sullen than overt. The Canadian news media were about as populist as a wet firecracker.

As the pain of increasing job losses mounts in Canada, ruining the lives of people and their families, ways will be found to express anger and to demand that the economic priorities of the country have to change. Particularly at the federal level, however, the formal political process is shackled in deadlock. The four major political parties in the House of Commons are focused almost exclusively on the short-term battle of position, against one another. Remarkably little creative thought is emanating from the parties. The Conservatives, Liberals, New Democrats, and Bloc Québécois have all become professionally run political organizations whose overwhelming interest is in institutional survival. For the Conservatives and Liberals, institutional well-being depends on achieving and holding office, and little else. The NDP and Bloc are caught up in the grinding struggle to win more seats when elections are held. Over the course of Canadian history, there have been many periods of creative politics when the energies of large numbers of people have transformed political parties into instruments to serve popular interests of one kind or another.

This is not one of those times. When we step back from the hurly-burly of partisan struggles, what stands out is the utter lack of imagination of Canada's political leaders when it comes to the need for a wholly new Canadian economic strategy that would build on the altered shape of the global economy. Still, political conditions can change rapidly, especially in a period of socio-economic crisis such as the one we are now experiencing. Movement and activist mobilizations could well create demands for change that become unstoppable.

Chapter Eleven

STAPLES, OIL SANDS, AND

OTHER RESOURCEFUL FANTASIES

WE CAN LOOK at the basics of the Canadian approach to the economy in any number of ways. Here (and in the following chapter) my choice is to focus on the role of Canada as a commodity-producing country and a manufacturer of transportation equipment—trains, planes, and automobiles. Even though the overwhelming majority of working Canadians are not employed in primary commodity production or in manufacturing, these two sectors have had, and continue to have, outsized roles in shaping the trajectory of the economy. What is especially remarkable, and deeply troubling, is how government approaches to these sectors have been totally inadequate, for much the same reasons over great spans of time.

For many decades economic historians, economists, and political economists have analyzed the reasons for Canada's centuries-old dependence on the production and extraction of primary products for export to economically more advanced nations. The famous staples thesis focuses on the appetites, first of Europeans, then of Americans and more recently of Asians, for access to Canadian primary products. Versions of the thesis highlight the establishment of commercial-communications linkages from a foreign metropolis—Paris, London, or New York—to Canadian metropolitan and satellite centres—Montreal, Toronto, Winnipeg, or Vancouver—to the ultimate source of the primary product in the wheat fields of the Prairies, the nickel mines of the Sudbury basin, or the oil sands deposits in the vicinity of Fort McMurray, Alberta.[1]

Other theories to explain the continued dependence of Canada on the export of primary products focus on the nature of the Canadian bourgeoisie and the relationship of its members with the capitalist classes in Britain and the United States.[2] Still others advance explanations that combine geographical determinism with the neoclassical theory of comparative advantage to conclude that in a world of open commerce, countries specialize in what they do best.

All of these approaches provide useful insights. But for me the greatest explanatory value comes in a thesis that combines the insights of the staples approach with an analysis of the relationship of the Canadian bourgeoisie with the bourgeoisie of more advanced countries. What is crucial to this narrative is the persistence over centuries of Canadian dependence on the production of primary products for export. The tendency for the Canadian state in its various elaborations, and the Canadian capitalist class in its different configurations, to emphasize the primary sector as crucial to Canadian economic strategy has endured for four centuries. The shifts from one primary product to another, driven by changing demand and evolving technology, are of great significance. But centrally important are the potential consequences of failing to seize the opportunity for advance during the present global crisis.

The long Canadian love affair with the export of primary products once again threatens to stand in the way of a creative response to the enormous challenges posed by the transformation of the global economy. Those at the helm of decision-making in Canada have been deeply invested with a set of choices on economic strategy that run counter to our interests today. Unless these choices are critiqued and effectively challenged, the prospects for our country globally are limited to a declining role, which means that the twenty-first century will by no means belong to us—to paraphrase Sir Wilfrid Laurier's conviction that the twentieth century would belong to Canada.

During this transition period a range of possible outcomes is possible. The country could end up in the first rank of countries in negotiating the changes, or it could fall to the second rank, which would mean a relative decline from the position the country has occupied since the end of the Second World War. The best-case scenario: Canada could be a Sweden, not in the size of its economy, but in its level of creative technological achievement. The worst-case scenario: Canada could move in the direction of an Argentina—and, remember, in the 1920s Argentina and Canada were perceived by analysts to be at about the same level of development and to have similar prospects for the future.

Unfortunately, the instincts of our political and business elites are much more likely to lead us towards the second outcome than the first. Centuries of dependency breed habits of mind that are not easily overcome. Those at the helm today are the descendants—if not genetically, then in every fibre of their being—of those who managed our affairs by clinging to their relationships with the centres of the imperial powers across the sea or south of the border. They are much more likely to think that selling the synthetic crude oil of the oil sands to the United States is a better idea than is rebuilding our cities and transportation equipment industries for the twenty-first century. With few exceptions, this is the kind of choice repeatedly made by those who have ruled Canada. It will be their choice once again if Canadians do not make an unholy row about it.

Unlike the Thirteen Colonies to the south, which during the eighteenth century developed metropolitan characteristics that threatened to make them competitors with the British rather than their compliant suppliers—a major cause of the American Revolution—the Canadian merchants in the first decades of the nineteenth century played the loyalty card and did not make much effort to step out of their appointed role. In sharp contrast to the leading people in the Thirteen Colonies, many of whom played a crucial part on the side of the revolutionaries, in Canada the leading people, the members of the so-called Château Clique in Montreal and the Family Compact in Toronto, fiercely opposed those who struggled for democracy, reform, and colonial autonomy. The united loyalty of the merchants and bankers on the side of the Crown was vital to the defeat of the forces of change and of the armed rebellions when they erupted in 1837–38.

The commercial elites in Canada clung to the benefits of the mercantile order until the British themselves, for reasons of their own, tore it to shreds in the late 1840s. By that date the British had negotiated the world's first Industrial Revolution, a transformation that significantly altered the nature of the British ruling class to include industrialists in addition to the traditional landed aristocrats and London-centred financiers. At the helm of the most competitive economic power in the world, the rulers of Britain were prepared to sell their goods everywhere and buy the timber and wheat they needed from whatever source was cheapest. The ideas of Adam Smith's *Wealth of Nations* made sense to them in a way they had not when the book had first been published in 1776.

The British repealed the Corn Laws and Navigation Acts and threw the British North American colonies out into the cold new world of classical economics.

The Canadian merchants and bankers were enraged by the new economics and the politics that went with it. In 1848 the British government instructed the Governor of Canada to concede one of the fundamental changes demanded by the reformers—Responsible Government. This meant that henceforth the Governor would allow his cabinet to be formed by those political leaders who enjoyed the support of the majority of members of the legislature's elected lower house. For the Tory commercial interests, this meant that the colonial government could now be led by the hated Reformers. In 1849 the Tories rioted in Montreal, at the time the capital of the Province of Canada. They burned down the legislative building and pelted the carriage of the Governor with rocks as he passed through the streets.

Also in 1849, leading members of the commercial class—including the Molsons and Torrances, Redpath, De Witt, Macpherson, Holton, Rose, and Workman—drew up a manifesto in which they called for the annexation of Canada by the United States. As the members of leading families in Montreal saw it, their loyalty to the Crown had been repaid with disdain, even betrayal. Unlike the Americans, who seized independence as the alternative to the disagreeable aspects of British rule, the Canadian ruling classes sought not independence, but annexation by the rising nation to the south.[3] They sought a new form of dependence as the key to their future well-being. It was a response to calamity that would recur over and over again in future times of crisis.

The merchant-banker class recovered from its fit of pique in subsequent years, not least because the British government negotiated a trade agreement with the United States that established a form of free trade between the United States and the British North American colonies. The key to this exchange would be the export of Canadian primary products to the United States and the export of U.S.-manufactured goods north. This reciprocity agreement pointed in the direction of the relationship that would prevail between Canada and the United States for much of the twentieth century.

The path to that relationship would not be straight and certain. Reciprocity was derailed by the American Civil War. Tensions arose between London and Washington especially after the British sold two warships to the Confederacy. In 1864 the U.S. government informed Britain that it was withdrawing from the Reciprocity Treaty. It gave the two years' notice stipulated for withdrawal in the treaty, which expired in 1866. For Canada's merchant-bankers, the end of reciprocity was a body blow. Exporting products to the United States had been an especially lucrative business during the war. For the second time, British North American business had its special commercial relationship, first with Britain and then with the United States, terminated by the other party.

The new course for the future grew out of Confederation, which was being promulgated by Canadian political leaders during the last years of reciprocity with the United States. The new Dominion of Canada, which came into existence on July 1, 1867, was the ideal state structure for the realization of a new economic strategy for Canadian business. What followed was indeed a long period of creative state and business activity in Canada.

For the first time the Canadian business class was pressured to act on a truly large scale to establish a viable transcontinental economy. In the late 1870s, while in opposition, Conservative leader

John A. Macdonald conceived the idea of a National Policy as a way of helping Canadian business cope with a recession that had hit North America and Europe. His idea was to sharply increase the tariffs on products being imported into Canada, particularly on manufactured goods. The goal was to promote import substitution. The tariff would make imported goods more expensive, which would in turn induce business to set up manufacturing operations in Canada to serve the Canadian market. That development would create jobs and staunch a huge flow of emigration from Canada to the United States. A year after Macdonald's Conservatives regained office in the election of 1878, the government implemented its new tariff strategy.[4]

While the tariff was the cornerstone of the National Policy, two other policies for national development were pursued by the federal government. Economic historians often analyze the other two policies—the completion of a transcontinental railway and state-sponsored immigration—as integral elements of the National Policy.

Macdonald lived to see the completion of the Canadian Pacific Railway in 1885, but not to see the prosperity he had hoped the National Policy would foster. That came in 1896, following the election of the Liberals to power under the leadership of Wilfrid Laurier, who had abandoned the old Liberal support for free trade in favour of the essential elements of the National Policy. With the lifting of the long recession, the return to prosperity in North America and Europe, and a sharp decrease in the cost of trans-Atlantic shipping as a consequence of newer and more efficient vessels, the Canadian economy surged forward.

Immigrants came to Canada from Europe and to a lesser extent from the United States to take up the offer of free land in the Prairie provinces, in the "last, best west." They added to the rising farm population of the region, which became the dynamic key to prosperity during these years. They grew the wheat that was transported east by the CPR and by ship to Europe. In the other direction, the transportation system brought immigrants and manufactured goods. The wheat economy drove the industrialization of Ontario and Quebec.[5] As a result of the tariff, Prairie farmers and other Canadians purchased an increasing proportion of their manufactured products, including farm machinery, from the factories of Central Canada. Western farmers, who had to sell their wheat in the unprotected global market, resented the National Policy tariff because it forced them to buy products from protected Central Canadian factories, and shut them off from importing cheaper goods from the United States. They charged, not without reason, that the real winners from the so-called National Policy were the bankers and railways based in Montreal and Toronto and the manufacturers of the East.

Despite its growing complexity, the Canadian economy still rested on the export of primary products, this time wheat, as the key spur to growth. The export of wheat and the increasing export of minerals, such as nickel, and of forest products financed the imported manufactured goods and paid for the construction of railways and harbours, the most important infrastructure projects of the era.

The great age of the National Policy was over by the time Canada had to cope with the new global arrangements of the postwar economy during the 1920s. The First World War overturned the existing global economic order in much the same way as the present economic crisis is transforming the global economy. At the end of that war the United States replaced Britain as the world's leading creditor nation, the most important source of capital for global economic development. With these new conditions in the 1920s, Canada's east-west economy and British orientation in trade and investment flows shifted to new north-south linkages between the United States and Canadian regions.

Primary products continued to be the key—nickel in Ontario, asbestos in Quebec, and forest products in New Brunswick, Ontario, and British Columbia. Exports of these products to the United States drove up provincial revenues and financed highway construction and the building of schools and hospitals. The political economy of Canada was shifting from a British to an American locus.

A crucially important case of resource mismanagement and shortsightedness—a precursor of the development of the petroleum industry in Alberta in recent decades—was the Ontario government's handling of the nickel industry.

Nickel was first mined on a significant scale in the late nineteenth century because its phenomenal hardening qualities made it crucial in an age when steel had become essential to a long list of industries. Structural steel to construct tall buildings and steel needed to build vast fleets of automobiles required nickel, and nickel was essential, as well, for the construction of ships, tanks, aircraft, and artillery shells, the *matériel* of the arms races and wars of the twentieth century.

By the end of the 1880s the U.S. navy was experimenting with nickel for use in the production of ship armour. During the naval arms race that preceded the First World War, the British, French, German, and U.S. navies required unprecedented amounts of nickel to build their warships.

The uniquely well-endowed nickel deposits of the Sudbury basin, which became the crucial centre of global nickel extraction in the early twentieth century, were discovered as a result of railway construction in the region in the late nineteenth century. Prior to the Ontario discovery, New Caledonia, a French penal colony in the South Pacific, was the world's leading source of the metal.

In 1902 the International Nickel Company was incorporated in the United States. J.P. Morgan and Company, the New York financial house that had recently organized the U.S. steel trust, created Inco. The newly established nickel company presided over the merger between the Orford Copper Company and the Canadian Copper Company, which gave it a dominant position in the Sudbury basin. Inco took over other companies, including Wharton's American Nickel Works, Vermilion Mining Company, Anglo-American Iron Company, Nickel Corporation of London, and the Société Minière Calédonienne.

Having established itself as the dominant producer, refiner, and marketer of nickel, enjoying close links with both the U.S. steel industry and U.S. government, Inco continued to push its monopoly advantage, achieving almost complete dominance of the world nickel industry. To put this in perspective, Inco and the Sudbury basin attained a far larger role in the global nickel industry than the Organization of Petroleum Exporting Countries (OPEC) ever has in the world petroleum industry.

The rise of Sudbury nickel led to a continuing debate in Ontario and federal politics about how to maximize the benefits for the country from its virtual world monopoly. The primary goal, both at Queen's Park and in Ottawa, was to maximize nickel production—over 90 per cent of it done for export. A secondary objective, supported at various times by the two levels of government, though not necessarily at the same time, was the promotion of nickel refining and nickel-based manufacturing in Canada.

The campaign to bolster manufacturing during this period achieved its greatest success with the establishment of Ontario Hydro as a publicly owned electric power generation and distribution system. The "public power" movement that created the political base for Hydro also generated support for the creation of a nickel-steel industry in Canada. Some of the supporters of this policy advocated public ownership as the means for its achievement.

During the First World War, Canadian public opinion turned strongly against Inco. The company was widely regarded as a "merchant of death" because it supplied vital war *matériel* to German industry. Canadians were especially enraged when they learned that the German submarine *Deutschland* had crossed the Atlantic during the war to pick up a cargo of nickel in the United States, which was not yet involved in the war. The nickel had been extracted in Canada, but refined in the United States.

Canadians concluded reasonably that Canadian nickel was being sold to Germany to produce weapons to kill Canadian soldiers. At the very least, an angry public demanded, Sudbury basin nickel ought to be refined in Canada. In September 1915 the government of Ontario appointed a commission, later changed to a royal commission, to report on the condition of the nickel industry and make recommendations for its future. In its report in March 1917, the Royal Ontario Nickel Commission concluded: nickel could be refined in Ontario on a cost-competitive basis; the Canadian nickel industry was the most productive and efficient in the world; governments should discount threats by nickel companies to shift production to other parts of the world—threats made in trying to avoid pressure to establish refining facilities in Canada;

and the government of Ontario should not drastically alter the taxation regime for the province's nickel industry.[6]

The conclusions of the royal commission were tepid, very much in line with the conclusions that the Alberta government reaches today when it considers the state of the petroleum industry in the province. The royal commission said yes to the viability of refining nickel in Ontario, but no to the idea of dramatically increasing the royalties that the industry had to pay the provincial government. Before the First World War and the storm over its sales of nickel to Germany, Inco had always maintained that it would be uneconomic to refine nickel in Ontario. The company insisted that its refinery in New Jersey was more efficient than an Ontario refinery would be, and that was because of the access in that state to cheaper supplies of fuels and chemicals. Inco regularly responded to pressure to build an Ontario nickel refinery by threatening to shut down its Sudbury basin mining operations in favour of the extraction of nickel in New Caledonia.

In response to the anger north of the border, however, Inco announced that it would build a nickel refinery at Port Colborne, Ontario, which it proceeded to do at the end of the war. Having escaped the threat of much higher royalties and the greater peril of nationalization, Inco went on to enjoy several decades of virtually complete dominance of the global nickel industry. In 1925 the company acquired the Anglo-Canadian Mining and Refining Company, a firm with British ties that had challenged Inco's monopoly at the end of the First World War. In 1928 another merger removed another competitor, the Mond Nickel Company, with its largely European markets. During the period from 1928 to the outbreak of the Second World War, Inco controlled between 80 and 90 per cent of the production of nickel in the non-Communist world.

Following the Second World War, Inco's monopoly position gradually eroded, and the proportion of global nickel output that it controlled began to decline. Within Canada the chief competition came from Falconbridge, which was incorporated in 1928. By the mid-1970s, even with Falconbridge as a competitor in the Sudbury basin, Inco still accounted for over 80 per cent of Canadian nickel production; but Canadian nickel production as a proportion of global output was dropping. By 1971 Canada was producing 54 per cent of the non-Communist world's nickel, and by the end of that decade just over one-third of the non-Communist world's nickel was extracted in Canada.

Despite its relative decline, Inco remained the world's largest producer of nickel, with its Sudbury basin operations still at the centre of its far-flung empire. As well as in Sudbury, Inco had Canadian nickel operations in the vicinity of Thompson, Manitoba, and in the area of Shebandowan, Ontario.

The shift in the global nickel industry to non-Canadian sources was accompanied by a shift in technology. The Canadian industry's specialty had been the production of class 1 refined nickel, the most expensive, high-grade variety of the metal. But the world nickel market was shifting to the cheaper class 2, less-refined nickel (75 per cent nickel matte). This cheaper source met the needs of the steel industry, which was also undergoing technological changes.

As Canada's nickel monopoly slipped away, so too did its historic opportunity to earn revenues that would create a capital pool to broaden the base of the regional economy of northern Ontario and other parts of Canada.

Canada's nickel strategy was short-sighted. Even when the country did enjoy its overwhelming monopoly, Queen's Park and Ottawa conceived of greater benefits from the industry largely by insisting on further processing and refining of nickel ore in Canada. This idea was the conventional wisdom in Canada. Simple extraction of the raw material, so the theory went, would lead first to further processing, and this step would then open the way for the production of sophisticated end products.

The problem with the theory was that it took little account of the crucial role of final demand for end products as the key element in determining the direction of economic development. End-product development for consumer products or for capital goods ultimately determined which raw materials would be extracted and in what quantity. Control at that end of the economic process was ultimately what mattered most, and Canada exercised little sway there because of the high degree of foreign ownership of the country's manufacturing sector. The idea of forward-processing of raw materials was a Canadian attempt to circumvent the problem of foreign ownership without really facing it. At best it led to Canadian exports not simply of raw primary products but of semi-fabricated products. It did not change the basic reliance of the Canadian economy on the production of raw materials for export.

In the case of nickel, some people had dreamed of what was fondly called "nickel-based manufacturing," which presumably meant the production of nickel end products in the country. The problem was that goods using nickel in their production have only a small percentage of the metal in the final product. The gigantic Canadian capacity to extract nickel and the very small proportion of nickel in end products meant that the strategy of forward-processing at home would never lead to "nickel-based manufacturing."

By 2006 Inco's Sudbury operations were producing only 10 per cent of the world's nickel, and in October of that year the Brazil-based Companhia Vale do Rio Doce purchased Inco for $19 billion. In 2009 the nickel industry, Sudbury in particular, was hit hard by a slump in base-metal prices. At the beginning of June Vale Inco shut down its mining and processing operations in Sudbury for eight weeks. On Monday, July 13, 3,100 Vale Inco workers went on strike in Sudbury, 85 per cent of them having voted to reject the company's latest contract offer. Issues in the strike included the pensions for new employees and the company's insistence on reducing a pay bonus linked to the price of nickel.[7] Like employees in other sectors, the Sudbury Inco workers reasoned that the costs of the recession were being unfairly unloaded on them. They were joined in the decision to strike by Vale Inco's employees in other smaller operations in Canada.

Canada's transition from a British-oriented to a U.S.-centred Canadian economy was only completed in the post–Second World War period. By the end of that war Canada lived in a global order that was completely different from the one that had existed three decades earlier. The United States occupied a unique position immediately following the war, producing 50 per cent of the goods and services in the entire world.

Towards the end of the war, the Liberal government of William Lyon Mackenzie King began planning for the transition to a peacetime economy, a transition overseen by C.D. Howe, a U.S.-born engineer and businessman who had sat in King's cabinet since 1935. Howe had been Canada's economic czar during the war, mobilizing the country's production of military vehicles, warplanes, ships, and equipment. When necessary, as it often was, he was quite prepared to create Crown corporations to do the job to overcome supply bottlenecks.

His vision for the peacetime economy was to dismantle wartime controls, sell off many of the Crown corporations, and open the door to new injections of foreign investment, which would come overwhelmingly from the United States. The King government in the postwar years conceived of Canada as a cornucopia of raw materials, a storehouse without limit, on which U.S. industry could draw. The tone is captured in postwar National Film Board documentaries about Canada's resources and forests. The message, entirely innocent of any basic concern about the environment, was that these resources held the key to the future for Canadians.

To be sure, the federal government wanted foreign investment in the manufacturing sector as well as in the resource sector. There was no concern in either case with the risk that the Canadian economy would largely end up controlled by outsiders, following six years of wartime growth of the country's industrial capacity, an achievement that flowed from the mobilization of domestic capital and a reduction of the proportion of industry owned by foreign companies.

What followed was the golden age of the branch-plant economy in Canada. U.S. firms poured capital into the resource sector and gained decisive control of mining, forestry, and the petroleum industry—with the development of that last sector taking off following the discovery of oil at Leduc, Alberta, in 1947. U.S. corporations also invested massively in the establishment of factories to produce manufactured goods. Most of that investment was made in southern Ontario, with a lesser amount going to the greater Montreal area.

What we can call the "branch-plant economic syndrome" emerged in the postwar years. It worked as follows: Canada's enormous export of primary products earned the country a vast surplus on that side of its commodity trade ledger; on the other side, Canada ran an enormous deficit on its manufacturing trade. The manufacturing trade deficit was built right into the branch-plant syndrome. The factories opened by U.S. firms in Canada produced goods for the domestic market, but they were almost entirely shut out of export markets. The branch plants were opened so that U.S. firms could gain access to Canadian consumers. Because of the tariff, a holdover from the old National Policy, the best way for U.S. corporations to gain access was to open manufacturing operations on the Canadian side of the border. When one U.S. manufacturing company opened a plant in Canada, that move placed pressure on its major competitors to do the same.

But the branch plants could not earn a trade surplus for Canada. That was because they imported the production machinery they used, usually from the United States, and they imported components used to assemble the products in Canada. Top management and research and product development were also based near head offices in the United States. The consequence was that when a Canadian consumer purchased a stove or a refrigerator with a "Made in Canada" sticker on it, that purchase increased Canada's manufacturing trade deficit. Branch-plant manufacturing, to use the term that was commonly used when all of this was analyzed critically in the late 1960s and early 1970s, was "truncated." It was unproductive in global terms, and could only exist as a consequence of the Canadian tariff. It was uncreative, and deployed hand-me-down technology from corporate head offices abroad. Among developed countries, Canada's research and development expenditures were among the lowest.

While initially the establishment of branch plants often involved the investment of new U.S. capital in Canada, once the subsidiary became profitable in Canada, company profits were remitted to the company's headquarters south of the border. The consequence was that this form of investment resulted over time in a net flow of capital out of Canada, not into Canada, as those who supported foreign investment liked to claim. Moreover, in many cases, the opening of a branch plant involved no new investment in Canada at all. Canadian banks were more than happy to lend money to U.S. corporations to open a plant in Canada or to take over an existing facility that was Canadian-owned. In such cases, foreign owners made use of Canadian capital to gain long-term control of Canadian plants. In cases in which foreign companies acquired ownership of Canadian plants by borrowing capital from Canadian banks, the net employment effect for Canada was negative. The U.S. firms typically supplied parts and components made in the United States to their Canadian subsidiaries; the components would likely have been manufactured in Canada had the firm been domestically owned.

The trade deficit that was built into the structure of branch-plant manufacturing also ensured that Canada would have to keep its exports of primary products as high as possible. Without those exports, the country would have had an unsustainable commodity trade and current account deficit. The paradoxical consequence of government support for the promotion of manufacturing through foreign ownership is that it forced policy-makers at both the federal and provincial levels to redouble their efforts to promote ever more primary products projects and exports.

The intimate link between the branch plants and the need for a high level of primary products exports was clearly understood by critics of Canadian economic policy by the early 1960s. The Watkins Report in 1968 and Gray Report in 1972 analyzed the dead-end course being taken by the Canadian economy.[8] By the time there was a rising tide of sentiment against foreign ownership and the costs of the branch-plant economy, Canada had opted for the Canada–U.S. Auto Pact as a solution to the specific problems of the auto sector.

If the quest for the beaver shaped the boundaries and extent of Canada, and wheat drew settlers to the Prairies and made a transcontinental Canadian state viable, petroleum raised Alberta to the status of a new Canadian metropolis and nurtured the dreams of oil barons and their political enablers.

Eastern bankers turned up their noses at Alberta petroleum in its early decades, which was one reason that the Alberta oil patch fell into the hands of the major U.S. and European oil companies. The Alberta oil industry came of age in 1947 with the discovery of the major oil field at Leduc just south of Edmonton by Imperial Oil, the country's largest petroleum company. Imperial was a subsidiary of Standard Oil of New Jersey (now Exxon Mobil), with 69.7 per cent of the company's stock held by Jersey Standard.

By 1960 non-residents owned 77.3 per cent of the investments in the Canadian petroleum industry. Foreign control of the industry was even higher, at 89.8 per cent. A decade later, foreign investment in the Canadian petroleum industry totalled $9.8 billion, and more than 91 per cent of the assets and more than 95 per cent of the industry's sales were accounted for by foreign-owned firms. Some 80 per cent of that foreign ownership was in the hands of major U.S.-based petroleum companies.[9]

During the 1960s and early 1970s, the basic goal of the Canadian subsidiaries of the foreign-owned petroleum companies was to increase the export of oil and natural gas to the United States. To stay in compliance with the regulations of the National Energy Board of Canada, which required that enough oil and natural gas be set aside for domestic needs, the companies issued reports making the case that Canadian petroleum reserves were ample for the domestic market for decades to come and that, therefore, Canada could safely increase its exports to the United States.

Then came the global oil price revolution of 1973, and things turned upside down with the quick and huge increase in the global price of oil. The Liberal government of Pierre Trudeau responded to the global petroleum crisis by establishing a regime of price controls and export taxes for the sale of Canadian oil. Under this regime, Ottawa froze the domestic price initially at $3.80 a barrel in September 1973. After the world price skyrocketed, the federal government raised the domestic price of petroleum to $6.50 a barrel. Meanwhile, Canadian oil was sold to the United States for the world price. The difference between the domestic price and the world price, for this exported oil, was collected by Ottawa in the form of an export tax.[10]

The Trudeau government's petroleum regime generated fierce opposition from the major oil companies, the governments of the petroleum-producing provinces (Alberta and Saskatchewan), and the U.S. government. The companies swiftly demonstrated that they had the means to fight the new regime. Prior to the global oil-price revolution, the companies, in their testimony before the

National Energy Board, had assured Ottawa that Canada had plenty of oil and natural gas to meet domestic needs for the long-term future. In 1972 Imperial Oil, making the case for additional exports of Canadian petroleum, included this statement in the company's annual report: "In the current debate, the export of Canada's energy resources is being questioned; in effect, we are being urged to 'bank' our petroleum resources. Our present energy reserves, using present technology, are sufficient for our requirements for several hundred years."[11] Just two years later, after Ottawa's pricing regime had been established, Imperial and the other petroleum giants sang a far different tune. In 1974, with their eyes firmly on the demolition of Canada's two-price system for petroleum (one for Canadians and another for Americans), the petroleum companies warned of looming oil and natural gas shortages that would come within a few years.[12] Gone were the surpluses that had supposedly existed as far as the eye could see.

By the time the oil companies claimed that they needed incentives to explore for the petroleum that Canadians would need in the not too distant future, the Trudeau government had become highly suspicious of the trustworthiness of the industry. Top ministers and officials had concluded that the information provided by the petroleum companies was heavily slanted to serve their own interests—which was one of the reasons that the Trudeau government decided to establish a publicly owned oil company, Petro-Canada. The NDP, which held the balance of power during the minority Parliament of 1972 to 1974, had pressured the Liberals to create a Crown-owned company. Before the election in summer 1974, in which the Liberals regained their majority, the government committed itself to create Petro-Canada. It was after the election, though, that major steps were taken to provide the company with a strong capital base

to take over the assets of a number of foreign-owned oil companies operating in Canada. Petro-Canada was to become a vertically
integrated company, operating in all aspects of the industry, from
exploration to production, refining, transporting, and retailing
petroleum products. Crucially, the company would provide a much-
needed "window on the industry" whose data on petroleum reserves
could be relied upon by the government.

In March 1975 Energy Minister Donald Macdonald made the
case in the House of Commons that Canada needed Petro-Canada
to deal with the vast changes that had roiled the petroleum industry: "It is the extent and nature of these changes which have in our
view tipped the balance decisively in favour of federal entrepre-
neurship in the oil and gas industries."[13]

Petro-Canada moved quickly to acquire the assets of foreign-
owned petroleum companies in Canada, under the Trudeau government, prior to its defeat in the election of 1979, and then again
following the Liberal victory in a second federal election in the
winter of 1980. Between 1976 and 1982 the Crown company purchased the Canadian assets of Atlantic Richfield, Phillips Petroleum, Petrofina Canada, and British Petroleum, spending $3.7
billion on these acquisitions.[14]

In 1980, following the resumption of power by the Liberals in
an election early that year—they had defeated the short-lived Conservative government of Joe Clark—the government introduced
the National Energy Program (NEP). Its centerpiece was the Cana-
dianization of the petroleum industry—the goal was 50 per cent
Canadian ownership by 1990—through both the growth of publicly owned Petro-Canada and the encouragement of privately
owned Canadian petroleum companies. Petro-Canada had already

been enlarged through numerous acquisitions of the assets of foreign-owned firms in Canada. The emphasis in the NEP was to foster the growth of privately owned Canadian firms through a tax-incentive scheme designed to further this objective. The Petroleum Incentive Program (PIP) established a tax system with higher rates for foreign-owned than for Canadian-owned petroleum companies. The additional taxes reaped from the foreign-owned companies were used as so-called PIP grants to provide additional capital for the Canadian-owned firms.[15]

The federal government retained its system of price controls, setting the domestic price of oil lower than the world price. In 1981 the federal government negotiated a revenue-sharing deal with the Alberta government. Tensions between the two governments remained high, however.

And then in 1982 the world price of oil plunged from about U.S.$30 a barrel to about $10 a barrel. The reasons for the collapse of petroleum at that time were not mysterious. The collapse resulted from the restoration of oil production in Iran—production had dropped perilously close to zero at the time of the Iranian Revolution in 1979, which had provoked a temporary doubling of the world price of oil.

With the onset of a sharp recession in 1982, and a surplus of oil production in the OPEC countries and from the North Sea, demand fell and so did the price. Alberta's jobless rate soared above the national average. Thousands of people turned to food banks to sustain themselves. In Calgary, newly constructed office towers were mothballed as projected business expansion turned to ashes.

At the time the Trudeau government was confidently forecasting an era of energy megaprojects that would propel the nation's economy forward as the world price of oil rose, according to some forecasts, to U.S.$60 a barrel. One attractive feature of the megaprojects for the members of the Trudeau government was that most of them would be located outside Alberta, in the Northwest Territories or the Beaufort Sea, or off the coast of Newfoundland in the Hibernia field, which was being explored at the time. Such massive developments would reduce the disproportionate power of Alberta in the energy politics of the country. They would induce capital investment, create jobs, and generate revenue for the federal government. When the price of oil fell, Ottawa's hopes disintegrated and the megaprojects vanished from the drawing boards and public discourse.

Along with many other petroleum-producing regions, such as Texas, which was equally hard hit—office towers were also mothballed in Houston—Alberta suffered during the years of the bust. In Alberta, though, a legend grew up (more truthfully it was concocted), and it persists to this day. According to the legend, the slowdown in the Alberta oil patch was caused by the Trudeau government's National Energy Policy.

When the price of oil fell, the petroleum companies sharply reduced their exploration activities in Alberta. As the province lapsed into a period of sharp recession, the myth spread like a prairie fire that the pain was caused by the NEP. The theory was established—based on no evidence—that interference from Ottawa had imperilled the well-being of the Alberta oil patch.

That myth served the interests of the foreign-owned oil companies, the U.S. government, and Conservative politicians who detested the idea of government involvement in the petroleum sector. Those who were not served by the myth were Canadians, in particular Albertans. Politicians looking for votes in Alberta are often tempted to attack the bogeyman of the NEP to curry favour in the province. The latest prominent politician to bash the NEP while speaking to Albertans was Liberal leader Ignatieff, who declared in February 2009 that Trudeau's energy policy had been a mistake.[16]

The trouble with the myth is that it has provided cover for the thoughtlessness and rapacity of energy policy in Alberta and in Ottawa over the past two decades or more. In 1984, when Brian Mulroney's Conservatives swept to power in a federal election, the new prime minister quickly travelled to New York to address the Economic Club and tell his corporate audience that Canada was "open for business" once again. The Mulroney government quickly ended the regulation of petroleum prices in Canada and dispensed with the National Energy Program. Instead of encouraging the growth of Canadian ownership in the petroleum industry, Mulroney sang the praises of foreign investment. He replaced the Trudeau-era Foreign Investment Revenue Agency (FIRA), which had been established to ensure that particular foreign takeovers of Canadian companies served the national interest, with Investment Canada, a body established to encourage foreign investments and takeovers.

The most important initiative that the Mulroney government took to ensure that no future Canadian government would ever attempt to do what the Trudeau government had done in the petroleum sector came under the heading of what was misleadingly labelled as "free trade." Under both the Canada–U.S. Free Trade Agreement (FTA) and later the North American Free Trade Agreement (NAFTA), negotiated with the United States by the Mulroney government, Canada's ability to control its own petroleum industry was dramatically curtailed.

The FTA, which came into effect on January 1, 1989, abolished the right of Canada to embark on a future NEP. Not only did it, in the "national treatment" provision, specify that Canada cannot tax Canadian and U.S. (later Mexican under NAFTA) companies at different rates, thereby negating a repeat of the PIP grant scheme, it also provided that Canada cannot institute a two-price petroleum policy, with a higher price for petroleum exported to the United States and a lower price for Canadians. On top of these measures, the trade agreement stipulated that Canada had to continue exporting as much petroleum to the United States as it had been exporting on a rolling average of the previous three years. This meant, among other things, that Canada would be required to continue its exports of petroleum to the United States even if imports of petroleum to Eastern Canada from overseas were cut off as a consequence of a supply crisis generated by falling supplies or a geopolitical conflict. This stipulation meant that Canada had to make the supplying of the U.S. petroleum market a higher priority than meeting the requirements of Canadian markets that were experiencing a shortage.

If, as the Harper government hoped prior to the economic meltdown, the opening of new oil sands projects dramatically increased Canadian petroleum production, the country's commitment to export more petroleum to the United States would rise in lockstep. The whole point of enlarged oil sands operations is to meet the oil requirements of the United States.

The petroleum provisions of the FTA and NAFTA compromise Canadian economic sovereignty more gravely than any previous undertaking ever made by a Canadian government. Significantly, Mexico, also a major exporter of petroleum to the United States, did not make a commitment to sustain the level of its oil shipments to that country. Moreover, Mexico retained its right to sell oil to U.S. purchasers at the world price while keeping domestic oil prices regulated at a lower level. Mexican nationalism would have made a Canadian-style energy deal with the United States politically inconceivable.

The provisions in the trade agreements that the Mulroney government negotiated were accepted without demur by both the Chrétien-Martin Liberal and the Harper Conservative governments. Canadians should recognize these agreements for what they are—"unequal treaties"—the phrase used by the Chinese to describe the treaties signed by China's governments with the great European powers during the nineteenth century.

To the extent that the Harper government has an economic policy in addition to its basic inclination to let the free market operate unhindered, it has been to make Canada an "energy superpower" in the twenty-first century. What this means is that Canada would export an increasing amount of oil and natural gas to the United States.

Already, over the past couple of decades the U.S. reliance on Canadian oil has grown steadily larger. In July 2006, at 1.6 million barrels a day, Canada was the largest single exporter of crude oil to the United States. Rounding out the top five exporters to the United States were Mexico, with just over 1.5 million barrels daily, Saudi Arabia, at over 1.2 million barrels, Venezuela, with nearly 1.2 million barrels, and Nigeria, with just over 1.0 million barrels. These five countries were the source of 66 per cent of U.S. oil imports.[17] What these totals make clear is the high dependence of the United States on Canada and other Western Hemisphere sources of oil and its relatively low reliance on Middle Eastern sources.

The Harper government's vision of Canada as a major world petroleum exporter is based on the Alberta oil sands. As oil, national security, and the war on terror have become tightly aligned in the thinking of U.S. political leaders, Washington has ever more closely scrutinized Canada's largest petroleum deposit, the oil sands. Located across an enormous region of northeastern Alberta—in three major areas spread over 140,800 square kilometres, an area larger than the state of Florida—centred on Fort McMurray about 300 kilometres north of Edmonton—the oil sands contain almost as much oil as the conventional reserves of Saudi Arabia.

In the early years of this century, oil sands investments totalled nearly $200 billion. By the spring of 2008, oil sands production reached 1.3 million barrels a day, more than half of Canada's oil production. Some 10 per cent of North American crude oil production already comes from the oil sands. Incredible as it may seem, the Alberta government produced one scenario: by 2050 the oil sands would produce eight million barrels of oil a day, transforming Alberta into a North American Saudi Arabia.[18]

The problem is that this oil is extremely expensive to extract, and producing oil from the oil sands involves strip-mining on a vast scale. Huge tracts of land will be reduced to a scarred horror. In addition, the production of oil from the oil sands requires enormous inputs of fresh water and natural gas. Moreover, the industrial process by which the oil is separated from the sand results in the release of large quantities of greenhouse gases into the atmosphere.

The oil sands have become by far the biggest source of emissions in Canada. It is no exaggeration to say that without a steep reduction in the production of synthetic crude oil from the oil sands, all other programs in Canada to reduce emissions will be fruitless. Oil sands development has directly shaped the environmental policies of the Harper government. In keeping with the lobbying position of the petroleum industry, which calls for what is euphemistically described as a "Made in Canada" policy, the

Harper government has repudiated Canada's pledge to live up to the Kyoto environmental accord to which it is committed.

The Harper government developed its policy approach at a time when oil prices were rising dramatically to a peak of U.S.$150 a barrel in the summer of 2008. As the oil price soared, the short-term economic prospects for the oil sands grew ever brighter. Capital investments by the companies in new oil sands projects skyrocketed. Calgary oil men and the members of the Harper government to whom they were closely tied looked forward to a time when Canada would be producing as much as four million barrels of oil a day, three-quarters of it from the oil sands. Most of this production would be transported by pipeline to U.S. refineries specifically geared to refining heavy, dirty synthetic crude.

As oil sands production increased, as did the number of projects to enable higher output in the future, Fort McMurray was bursting with new development. The city's labour shortage pushed up wages and the demand for workers, who flooded in from across the country. Weekly non-stop flights from St. John's, Newfoundland, to Fort McMurray imported workers to toil at oil sands projects and then took them home a few weeks later, full of good cheer, their wallets bursting with the earnings to spend when they got back home. There were thousands of new jobs in the city: constructing houses, roads, shopping centres, and schools. The province hired crews to improve the notoriously dangerous highway from Edmonton to Fort McMurray.

The rise of Fort McMurray and the oil sands also had immediately damaging consequences for other regions of the country. For one thing, as the price of oil rose and investments flowed into the oil sands, the Canadian dollar took off on a tear against the U.S. greenback, peaking at U.S.$1.10 in the early autumn of 2007. The pace of the dollar's acceleration hurt other sectors of the economy, particularly the manufacturing sector. The price of labour, relative to that in other countries, rose so fast that industries had little time to adapt to the shock. The auto industry and the industries that supplied it were casualties, as were the publishing industry and the nation's booksellers.

In the boom atmosphere of the times these costs to other industries seemed minor in comparison to the new wealth flowing from a single sector. Later, when the global economy crashed, it would be seen that numerous industries were dangerously weakened on the eve of Canada's descent into economic malaise.

Those who approve of Canada's recent approach to economic policy-making would make the argument that it has always been the case that one booming sector could derail other sectors, drawing labour away from them and pushing up their costs. What matters, they have argued and continue to argue, is the overall performance of the economy. The Canadian story has always been one of rising and falling sectors. It is not the job of government to try to pick winning sectors; that is the job of the market.

The price of oil began to plunge from its high in the summer of 2008 to a low of just over U.S.$40 a barrel by the end of the year, before it began to climb again in the spring of 2009. The collapse of the price of oil was a consequence of the general economic collapse. As with the storms that have washed the rainbows out of the skies of previous resource booms in Canada, the transition from boom to bust had its genesis outside Canada. New oil sands investments dried up quickly as the economic downturn took hold.

Alberta's economy was hard hit by job losses and lagging output.

There are two ways of eliminating NAFTA's intolerable intrusions into Canadian sovereignty in the future. The first would be by renegotiating NAFTA with the United States and Mexico to remove the offending clauses. The second would be by giving notice under the terms of NAFTA that Canada intends to withdraw from that agreement.

Alternatively, if we retain the policy framework we have had in Alberta and at the federal level over the past quarter-century, what can we expect in the future from our petroleum industry? For the immediate future, as long as oil prices remain relatively low, not a great deal of capital will flow into financing new oil sands projects. It is enormously more costly to produce synthetic crude oil in the oil sands than it is to extract it from the huge conventional fields of the Persian Gulf. Only when world prices rise substantially can we expect robust investments to resume in the oil sands. That can be expected when the global economic crisis is succeeded by a resumption of growth.

With the Conservatives at the helm, or the Ignatieff Liberals for that matter, the agenda will remain the same as during the last boom. Along with rising oil prices, we can expect the Canadian dollar to rise once again against the U.S. dollar, which is bound to delay the recovery of the manufacturing sector and could even block the extent of its recovery. As exports of oil to the United States then rise, so too will Canada's NAFTA obligation to sustain the higher level of exports for the long term. Canada, as so often before over the centuries, will set forth on a course of development based on the excessive export of primary products at the expense of all else.

Alberta, which has had a right-wing government, with one change of party label, since 1935, will go on selling its oil while

collecting peanuts for this in relation to the royalties collected elsewhere. With roughly the same population as Alberta, Norway has
accumulated more than U.S.$260 billion from the sale of its North
Sea oil production, compared to the $15 billion that Alberta has
put aside.[19] Norway's capital is not used to defray current government costs. It is invested to generate economic development in
Norway long after its own oil reserves are depleted.

Canada's approach to primary resources and the rewards that
flow from them has always emphasized the immediate gratification of getting new projects up and running. Governments have
encouraged resource development, making few demands on business to pay high royalties and to clean up the environmental mess
they make. In the case of the forest products industry, the policies
have allowed companies to mine forests and placed little emphasis
on serious silviculture. Mining companies have paid low royalties
and created massive environmental damage.

The tales of the nickel industry during the twentieth century
and of the petroleum industry today are classic cases of the dead-
end Canadian approach to resource development. The country
continues to do what it has done for four centuries—export the sta-
ple products that other countries need without figuring out how to
use the resources to further our own development qualitatively.

The approach of both the Conservatives and the Liberals to the
crash is to wait for the Americans to get their act together so that
demand for Canadian commodities will increase and our economy
can recover. It is the old Canadian way, tried and not so true. It
leads the country from one horizon to the next, but never to the
promised land of qualitatively more advanced economic development. Those who have not learned the lessons of their country's
economic history are condemned to go on repeating the past.

Chapter Twelve

TRAINS, PLANES,
AND AUTOMOBILES FOR
TWENTY-FIRST-CENTURY CANADA

———————————

SAILING VESSELS and canoes drove the first Canadian economies, those of the fishery and the fur trade. In these vessels Europeans journeyed to the Grand Banks of Newfoundland and along the great waterways of the northern half of the continent in the quest for profitable commerce. In the early decades of the nineteenth century, canals cheapened the passage of goods on the Great Lakes and the St. Lawrence and made Montreal the leading centre of Canadian commerce. In the middle of the century, railways revolutionized life and played an enormous role in the creation of a fledgling Canadian nation that spanned the continent. Railways underpinned the new Canadian state, an east-west economy, and the export of wheat from the Prairies to Europe, making Canada an economic success with a rapidly rising population by the first decade of the twentieth century.[1]

The first mass age of the automobile in Canada came in the 1920s, as provincial governments built the nation's initial highways. It was not until the 1950s, following decades of depression and war that the automobile became a means of transportation for most Canadian families. Over the space of a few decades, governments built superhighways and the Trans-Canada Highway. Suburbs, relying on the automobile as the crucial form of transportation, exploded outwards from the cities. Urban density fell as city dwellers shifted from public transit to their cars. The public saw expressways as symbols of progress. One of them, the notorious Gardiner Expressway in Toronto, cut the city off from its lakefront. It was not until the 1970s, not coincidentally a decade when the price of petroleum exploded, that city dwellers perceived the downside of expressways that tore up neighbourhoods. In Toronto, public pressure stopped the building of the planned Spadina Expressway.

The initial era of skyrocketing petroleum prices lasted from 1973 to 1982. From 1982, when prices plunged, until the early years of the twenty-first century, petroleum was once again cheap, and Canadians, in company with Americans, purchased vast numbers of suvs, vans, pickup trucks, and recreation vehicles, all vehicles with poor gas mileage. The rising price of petroleum during this decade, coupled with the bursting of the global property price bubble beginning in the United States and the onset of a global economic crisis, plunged Canadians into a new world of transportation issues.

With an inefficient fleet of automobiles, poor public transit, an ailing rail system, and airlines plagued with a host of problems, Canada is woefully ill prepared for a transportation revolution. For a country whose vast size and low population have always made transportation a vital matter, the lack of planning by governments and industry to prepare for the dramatic changes in transportation has been flagrant, not to say negligent.

What Canada needs is an approach to transportation equipment industries that is integrated, not only so that autos, rail, and aircraft can play their roles effectively, but also so that the transportation sectors are developed in conjunction with the other major changes underway. Along with the economic crisis that confronts us, we are living in a time when the pressures of climate change and peak oil—the passing of the age of readily accessible petroleum on a scale sufficient to meet global needs—are forcing industrial societies to rebuild their cities along with their transportation systems and transportation equipment industries. Among the transformations we can anticipate in Canada and other industrialized countries are:

- the decline of the suburb and a return to the more densely populated urban patterns of earlier times;
- the closing of the centres of large metropolises to private automobiles, in favour of tramways, subways, and taxis;
- the elimination of air travel for distances of less than 500 kilometres in substantially populated regions and the replacement of short-haul flights by high-speed trains;
- the decline of truck transport for long routes and the rebuilding of rail lines to take up a much larger share of the shipment of freight; the demise of suvs, recreational vehicles (rvs), and cars with more than four cylinders; the long-term replacement of traditional autos by hybrids and zero emission vehicles (zevs), including those propelled by electric batteries and hydrogen. (As an energy carrier, not an energy source, hydrogen relies ultimately on other forms of power generation.)

The Canadian experience with the automobile industry is highly significant, among other things, because it has been emblematic of the country's inadequate approach to industrial development. If the lessons of the first century of auto production in Canada are not learned—and there are few signs that governments and political leaders have learned them—the prospects for the industry in Canada in coming years are grim indeed.

For half a century the risk of catastrophe has loomed over the auto industry in Canada—and over those who work in the plants, and their families and the communities they live in. Though it was not possible to predict when and in what precise form a transforming crisis would strike, the calamity that has now befallen the industry and that threatens its future was entirely predictable. The critical decision that pointed Canada's auto industry towards this doleful time was made in the 1960s, but its antecedents went back further to the beginning of the twentieth century.

Since the first decade of the twentieth century, Ontario has prospered as a consequence of the location in its cities of an automotive industry, large enough to be globally significant. From the eastern edge of the Golden Horseshoe to 400 kilometres westward in Windsor, southern Ontario is home to over half of Canada's manufacturing and an even higher proportion of the nation's heavy manufacturing. The jewel in the crown of Ontario manufacturing, which also includes steel, chemicals, and electronics, is the auto industry. Directly and indirectly, hundreds of thousands of jobs in Ontario are linked to auto manufacturing.

The first automakers in Ontario were Canadian. The most famous was Oshawa's Sam McLaughlin, who made the leap from manufacturing horse-drawn carriages to producing the horseless variety. Because he could not manufacture engines as cost-effectively as the Americans could, McLaughlin began importing Buick and Chevrolet engines from Detroit. In 1904 Henry Ford opened a factory in Windsor, across the river from his Detroit operations, to manufacture cars.

Just over a decade later, McLaughlin sold his Chevrolet and Buick operations to General Motors, leading in 1919 to the establishment of General Motors of Canada. During the 1920s the U.S. Big Three, GM, Ford, and Chrysler, found it profitable to assemble vehicles in Canada, both for the Canadian market and for export to other British Empire countries. Locating plants in Canada permitted the Big Three to skirt around Canada's high tariffs on imported manufactured products. In addition, autos produced in Canada were eligible for the low-tariff advantage known as British Preference when they were shipped to other countries in the Empire. This phase in the history of the Canadian auto industry peaked in 1929, when the country's automakers produced 263,000 vehicles, 102,000 of them for export.

The Great Depression that followed the stock market crash of 1929 slammed the door shut on this first golden age in the history of the Canadian automotive industry. By 1933, domestic auto production had plunged to 40,000 vehicles annually. Although auto production increased from this low during the rest of the decade, it did not get close to the 1929 level. During the Second World War, production of civilian vehicles was halted altogether. Instead the auto industry turned its attention to the production of military vehicles.[2]

When civilian auto production resumed after the end of the war, the Canadian auto industry functioned in a global environment far different from that of the 1920s. In the 1950s the market for automobiles expanded enormously in North America and

Western Europe. Fiat, Volkswagen, Renault, and Peugeot grew swiftly in Italy, West Germany, and France. British plants were turning out Austins. In Sweden, a potentially important role model for Canada as a small country producing its own cars, there were two national companies, Volvo and Saab. Beginning to emerge during these years were Honda, Nissan, and Toyota, the Japanese auto producers that would grow to dominate much of the global auto market in coming decades.

The Canadian subsidiaries of the Big Three U.S. producers no longer had access to their former export markets in British Empire/Commonwealth countries. Limited to the Canadian domestic market, they had become "miniature replicas" of the operations of the Big Three in the United States. They were hampered by all of the problems of branch-plant manufacturing. The vehicles they produced were conceived and designed in the United States, where top management was located.

Almost all of the production machinery deployed in the Canadian plants was produced south of the border. Most of the engines and sub-assemblies and many of the parts and components used in the production of autos in Canada were imported from the United States. In addition, the Canadian auto assembly plants of the Big Three could not match the economies of scale of their U.S. operations. That was because, while the production run for a single auto could total 300,000 vehicles in the United States, the Canadian domestic run for the same model was in the range of 30,000 vehicles. This meant that the U.S. plants could achieve a ratio of fixed to variable costs that the Canadian plants could not hope to match.

By 1960 all of these factors had come together to create a chronic malaise for the industry. Canada was importing far more finished vehicles than it was exporting. The largest single source of these vehicles was Britain, whose automakers shipped 80,000 vehicles annually to Canada. When to this was added the import of engines, sub-assemblies, and parts, Canada was saddled with a serious negative trade balance in the auto sector. The relatively small Canadian auto-parts sector supplied only a limited portion of the parts requirements of the assembly plants. The wages of Canadian auto workers were significantly lower than the pay of U.S. auto workers.

In the late 1950s the number of jobs in the Canadian auto industry was falling, from 33,428 in 1955 to 27,683 in 1960.[3] During the economic downturn at the end of the 1950s, John Diefenbaker's Conservative government established a one-man royal commission, headed by economist Vincent Bladen, to consider the options for the auto industry. While the royal commission report in 1961 did succeed in analyzing the ills of the industry, its recommendations had little to do with the future evolution of the industry.

Over the next few years two broadly divergent options dominated the debate. The first option was that Canada should follow the lead of European auto-producing countries and manufacture vehicles primarily for the Canadian domestic market. The second option, which would become the basis for future government policy, was that Canada should integrate its auto-production facilities with auto manufacturing in the United States: following a trade agreement in the auto sector, the Canadian plants would produce for segments of the continental market. Both choices had their champions. Key locals of the Canadian section of the United Auto Workers (UAW) and a sizeable number of Canadian-owned auto-parts producers backed the first option. The Big Three auto manufacturers and the Canadian region of the UAW were on the side of continental integration.

The choice that the Liberal government of Lester Pearson ultimately made was that of continental integration of the auto industry. The concern the government had with that choice was that
General Motors, Ford, and Chrysler were U.S.-owned companies,
and so too were many of the major parts suppliers for the Canadian
auto industry. The problem was that at some critical point in the
future, perhaps in the midst of a severe economic crisis, decisions
might be taken in the United States that would be deeply injurious
to Canadian interests.

In 1964 the Pearson government negotiated the Canada-U.S.
Auto Pact with the Johnson administration in Washington. The
pact came into force in 1965. A sectoral trade agreement, the Auto
Pact differed in essential ways from the later Canada-U.S. Free
Trade Agreement and NAFTA. It allowed the Big Three automakers
and the producers of original auto parts (parts included in vehicles
at the time of purchase) to ship their products duty-free in either
direction across the Canada-U.S. border provided certain commitments were met. The reason for the inclusion of these commitments, known as safeguards, was that the Canadian government
insisted that because the auto companies were U.S.-owned, Canada
needed a guarantee that significant auto production would continue north of the border once the Auto Pact went into effect.
The first safeguard, which was easily met and swiftly became
unimportant, was that companies had to match or exceed the dollar value of their production in Canada in 1964 to be eligible for
duty-free treatment of their shipments. The second safeguard—
the one that really mattered—was that as the market for cars and
trucks increased in Canada, the production in Canada had to
increase as well. In the case of cars, every additional dollar's worth
of sales that a company made had to be matched by at least sixty

cents' worth of additional production in Canada, or of "Canadian Value Added," the term that was used. In the case of trucks, every additional dollar's worth of sales had to be matched by at least fifty cents' worth of additional Canadian Value Added.

While the Auto Pact covered original auto parts, it did not cover replacement parts—the parts that needed to be replaced in vehicles when car owners made repairs. The replacement-parts market in Canada continued to be sheltered against imports from the United States through the imposition of a 15 per cent tariff.

Within a few years of the implementation of the Auto Pact, the auto plants in Canada were retooled to produce products for segments of the North American market rather than simply for the Canadian market. Once this process of reordering its production was complete, Canada's Big Three exported about 60 per cent of the vehicles they assembled to the United States. Most of the Big Three vehicles purchased by Canadians were assembled south of the border.

The Auto Pact established a gigantic two-way trade in assembled vehicles and auto parts across the Canada-U.S. border, with its locus the border-crossing points between Detroit and Windsor, although other border-crossing points between Ontario and the United States were also important. A pattern in this trade was established right from the start, and this pattern persisted throughout the life of the Auto Pact, during the good years and the bad, and even after the agreement ceased to function. Canada's exports of assembled vehicles to the United States were much larger in value than were Canada's imports of assembled vehicles from south of the border. On the other hand, Canada imported a much greater dollar value's worth of auto parts from the United States than the value of its parts exports to that country. Except for a few years in the early 1970s, when Canada's overall trade in assembled vehicles and parts under the Auto Pact lapsed into deficit, Canada's auto trade with the United States became the source of a persistent and growing trade surplus.

One of the most important reasons for the trade surplus was the long-term decline in the value of the Canadian dollar against the U.S. dollar. In the mid-1960s, when the Auto Pact went into effect, the Canadian and U.S. dollars were of roughly equal value. Both the governments signing the pact and the auto companies assumed that wage costs would be similar in Canada and the United States. As the value of the Canadian dollar slid against the U.S. dollar after the mid-1970s, for the auto companies the cost of labour in Canada became lower than the cost of labour south of the border. For instance, when the Canadian dollar was at eighty cents against the U.S. dollar, the labour costs of auto companies in Canada were effectively 20 per cent lower than in the United States, even if the nominal rate of pay was the same in the two countries. Another major reason Canada did well under the Auto Pact in attracting the investments of the Big Three was that in Canada medicare covered the health-care costs of employees. In the United States, the auto companies had to provide billions of dollars in health-care benefits to their employees. Moreover, autoworkers in Canada had a better on-the-job record, with lower rates of absenteeism and less sabotage of company equipment compared to their U.S. counterparts. Finally, the Big Three continued to charge more for their vehicles in Canada than did their counterparts south of the border, even after exchange rates and tax rates were taken into account. As a consequence of all of these factors, the auto companies made higher profits on the vehicles they assembled in Canada. Over the period that the Auto Pact functioned as originally designed, from 1965 to

1989, the number of workers employed by the auto industry in Canada, with ups and downs along the way, grew from 83,000 to 155,000.[4]

As the technology advanced, the companies developed just-in-time delivery of the components needed for vehicles in the assembly plants. Each vehicle differed in substantial ways from the one in front of it or behind it on the assembly floor. Parts and components arrived at the plants only an hour or even less before they were installed in vehicles. On the floors of the plants where this high-tech assembly was in operation, almost none of the production machinery had been made in Canada. Once, when I visited a GM plant in Oshawa in the late 1990s, I saw workers who were no longer tied to an assembly line. They were working in gangs on automobiles brought to them on driverless vehicles that moved the product from station to station. The machinery in the plant, including these robotic vehicles, was designed and produced in Sweden, other European countries, the United States, and Japan. When I visited the assembly line for Chrysler vans in Windsor, I saw robots doing jobs formerly done by hundreds of workers. The robots were also not made in Canada. Still, as long as nothing fundamental changed, the industry in Canada would retain its strong position, despite the underlying weaknesses.

Throughout the history of the Auto Pact, European and later Asian automakers were carving out markets for their vehicles in Canada—although this was something that did not seem especially significant in the early years, Even before the Auto Pact, in the late 1950s, those odd little Volkswagen Beetles were putting in an appearance on Canadian streets. By the early 1970s, Japanese vehicles were being unloaded off ships for sale in Canada. Over time the European and Asian automakers gained an ever larger market share in Canada and the United States. Moving out from exports, the leading Japanese automakers—Toyota, Nissan, and Honda—began producing cars in North America on both sides of the border. Based in plants in Tennessee and Ontario, these producers were cutting deeply into the market shares of the Big Three.

The FTA and NAFTA effectively killed the Auto Pact. While the Auto Pact was a sectoral-managed trade deal, the FTA and NAFTA were free-trade agreements formulated in accordance with a neo-liberal free-market ideology. As tariffs were quickly reduced to zero between Canada and the United States, and later Mexico, the safeguard that guaranteed a minimum level of production in Canada—the reimposition of the tariff in the event of a fall of production by one or more automaker—was removed.

By the mid-1990s the Auto Pact no longer functioned to regulate the production of vehicles produced by the Big Three in Canada in relation to the market size of GM, Ford, and Chrysler in Canada. Instead, it was used as a mechanism to protect North American auto producers from European and Asian competitors. The Pact was used to allow duty-free shipments both ways across the border for vehicles that contained at least 50 per cent North American content—that is, content that resulted from production in either Canada or the United States.

From the beginning of the North American content regime, European and Asian automakers made the case that the revised Auto Pact resulted in discrimination against them under the rules of the World Trade Organization (WTO). In 2000 a WTO panel ruled that the Auto Pact did indeed discriminate against these auto producers. As a consequence, the Auto Pact ceased to exist in any form.[5]

By the time of the WTO ruling the role of auto producers from outside North America, especially from Asia, had transformed the market for vehicles in Canada, as well as the production of automotive products in Canada. By 2005, 32.5 per cent of vehicles purchased in Canada—a total of 514,000 units—were being produced by Japanese-owned auto companies. That same year the combined output of assembled vehicles in Canada at the plants of Honda, Toyota, and CAMI (a joint venture of the Japanese-owned Suzuki Motor Corporation and GM Canada) totalled 881,000. Of these units, 721,000 were exported, with 95 per cent of these exports going to the United States. Considerably more Japanese cars were assembled in Canada than were purchased in Canada, then, and most of the Japanese cars purchased in Canada were assembled elsewhere: in Japan, the United States, or Mexico. Some eleven thousand workers were employed in the three motor vehicle plants operated in Ontario by the Japanese auto companies. In 2005 the four bestselling vehicles in Canada—Honda Civic, Mazda3, Toyota Corolla, and Toyota Echo—were all produced by Japanese firms. The fifth bestselling car in Canada, the Ford Focus, was the top seller among the Big Three automakers.[6]

In recent years the auto industry in Canada was hit with a new series of basic problems that have set the stage for the future, with two challenges in particular emerging side by side: the dramatic rise in the value of the Canadian dollar against the U.S. dollar; and the skyrocketing price of gasoline. The swift climb of the Canadian dollar, which soared past the U.S. dollar in value for a few months in 2007, made the price of labour in Canada much higher in relation to labour south of the border. The auto companies had enjoyed the cushion of cheaper labour at their Canadian plants for decades. Suddenly this cushion was wrenched away from them. Meanwhile, as gasoline prices spiked, automobiles sales turned soft. Then came the financial meltdown, the stock market crash, and the onset of the economic crisis. The fall of gasoline prices, which would have been welcome earlier, did little to revive auto sales.

By the time of the crash of 2008 the Canadian auto sector had already been bled to the point of terminal weakness. The Big Three, especially General Motors and Chrysler, faced the necessity of total restructuring and downsizing and the very real possibility of declaring bankruptcy. In the United States, too, the fate of the Big Three—though Ford was somewhat healthier because of its relatively strong cash position—was effectively in the hands of the Obama administration.

Even before the Bush administration left office, the top executives of the Big Three were making the case in Washington that they desperately required government assistance, to the tune of about U.S.$25 billion. On November 18, 2008, the CEOs—Rick Wagoner of GM, Alan Mulally of Ford, and Robert Nardelli of Chrysler—flew to Washington in their corporate jets, Wagoner in GM's luxurious $36-million aircraft, to tell members of Congress why they needed billions of dollars from the federal government. The optics of supplicants arriving in such wasteful opulence made a bad impression on lawmakers who were already getting negative feedback about corporate bailouts from their constituents.[7]

By late March 2009, when the White House acted on the imminent prospect of GM and Chrysler having to declare bankruptcy, the administration had spent weeks dealing with the populist backlash that swept the country in the wake of the payments of bonuses to AIG executives. This time the administration was determined to play tough with the two ailing auto giants. The Obama auto team forced Wagoner to step down as a CEO of GM as a condition of considering a bailout for the company. The team, having concluded that Chrysler was not viable on its own, was prepared to lend cash to the company for a thirty-day period to allow it to seek a corporate alliance with Italy's Fiat. Should the deal with Fiat fall through, the administration saw bankruptcy as the only option. Similarly, should GM fail to come up with a suitable plan for its restructuring within sixty days, the company would have to file for bankruptcy protection. Obama's auto team announced that given the grim circumstances they faced, both companies "may well require utilizing the bankruptcy code in a quick and surgical way."[8]

In this critical situation, the Canadian and Ontario governments were exposed as utterly impotent, unable to do anything except to repeat what Obama was saying. On March 30, Obama announced his position on GM and Chrysler to the media. "Our auto industry is not moving in the right direction fast enough to succeed," he warned. But the president also set out his vision of the industry's future: "I am absolutely committed to working with Congress and the auto companies to meet one goal: The United States of America will lead the world in building the next generation of clean cars."[9]

A couple of hours after Obama's White House announcement, Canada's Industry minister, Tony Clement, put a brave face on, saying exactly what the president had said. Chrysler had thirty days to make a deal with Fiat, and GM had sixty days to work out its plans for the future. "The plans don't go far enough," Clement said of the efforts of the two companies to date. "There is some fundamental restructuring that must take place." He announced a short-term $1 billion loan to Chrysler with a $250-million installment within days to allow the company to meet its payroll obligations.

The same day, in a televised news conference, Finance Minister Jim Flaherty and Ontario Economic Development Minister

Michael Bryant announced that the two governments would lend $3 billion to General Motors to assist the company in launching its restructuring effort, one-third of this coming from Queen's Park. Flaherty told reporters separately that the leaders of the Canadian Auto Workers (CAW) needed to do more on compensation in order to make Chrysler and GM competitive.

"This is very serious and I encourage the union leadership very seriously to go back and speak with management," Flaherty said. "This isn't about collective bargaining; this is about saving thousands of jobs in Ontario and in Canada."

During the month of April 2009 a multi-sided power struggle, or game of chicken, took shape over the future of Chrysler. The Obama administration, echoed by Ottawa, took the position that the United States and Canada would not pour funds into Chrysler unless the ailing company was able to reach a merger arrangement with Fiat. This public stance gave Fiat the whip hand, and the Italian automaker proceeded to use it. Fiat made it clear that unless wages and benefits were drastically reduced at Chrysler Canada, by about $19 an hour, there would be no deal. Sergio Marchionne, Fiat's chief executive officer, told *The Globe and Mail* that workers on both sides of the Canada-U.S. border would have to abandon their sense of entitlement. He added that the CAW had taken "more rigid positions" than the UAW.[10]

In this power struggle, Industry Minister Clement wholeheartedly took the side of Fiat against Chrysler's Canadian workers and the CAW. Clement told *The Globe and Mail* that he had spoken to the Fiat CEO and that the car executive was unequivocal that he would walk away from Chrysler if labour costs in Canada and the United States were not dramatically reduced. "It's not pleasant, it's not palatable to the union, I understand that," Clement said. "But we cannot have a situation where the union is resisting the reality of the situation and then expecting the Canadian taxpayers and the Ontario taxpayers to contribute." With no Fiat deal, Clement said, there would be no further loans to Chrysler.

The minister was adding the weight of the government to that of Fiat in negotiating with the CAW. He told the CBC that it was not his role to be involved in the bargaining process, technically between Chrysler and the CAW but realistically between Fiat and the CAW. Clement was being completely disingenuous. He was twisting the arm of the CAW on behalf of Fiat, and he knew it. He was signalling to Fiat that the company should not back off on its full demands where the workers were concerned. More than that, in the event that Chrysler ended up with no deal with Fiat, and did declare bankruptcy, he and the other members of the Harper government had their scapegoat: the autoworkers and their union. Should the plan to rescue Chrysler succeed, at least in the short-term, the anti-union Conservatives would have attained one of their goals, the weakening of the CAW, Canada's most effective industrial union.

By rights the issue of worker compensation has to be tightly connected to the profitability of the Canadian operations of General Motors and Chrysler. A study on auto company profitability by CAW economist Jim Stanford concluded that between them the two companies realized profits of \$37 billion between 1972 and 2007. The study showed that the two automakers generated profits on their operations in Canada every year for the period studied except for 2002. GM's overall profit for the thirty-five-year period was \$31.75 billion; Chrysler's was \$4.95 billion.

"And even in the years from 2005 through 2007, when the U.S. auto industry slid deeply into red ink, the Canadian industry remained profitable," Stanford concluded. Stanford's analysis of the companies' profits was made by combining data they publicly released before 1996, with figures since then extracted from Statistics Canada data for the whole industry.[11]

For their part GM and Chrysler were seeking loans in Canada that were proportional, given the scale of their Canadian production operations, to the loans being sought in the United States. General Motors wanted up to $7.5 billion, and Chrysler was seeking about $4 billion.[12]

In the end, in the United States first Chrysler and then General Motors declared bankruptcy. A feverish effort to avoid bankruptcy for Chrysler ended in failure on the afternoon of April 30, 2009, the deadline set by the Obama administration for an agreement to be reached on restructuring the company's debt. Ironically, after all the public pressure directed at the UAW and the CAW, it was the unwillingness of some of the companies' hedge-fund creditors to make a deal that forced Chrysler to seek bankruptcy protection. Obama was sharply critical of the investors who stood in the way of a deal. "I don't stand with them," he declared. "I stand with Chrysler's employees and their families and communities. I don't stand with those who held out when everybody else is making sacrifices."[13]

All of Chrysler's U.S. plants were closed until further notice, putting its 94,000 employees on a leave of unspecified duration. In Canada, Chrysler plants in Windsor and Brampton were idled. On the day when Chrysler declared bankruptcy, it also signed a deal with Fiat that allowed the Italian auto producer to acquire a 20 per cent equity stake in the company. Effectively, this agreement put Fiat in charge of Chrysler for the future. Even though the UAW was to retain a 55 per cent share in the company, this share operated through the trust that managed the health care of company retirees.

The classification of the UAW's stock meant that it would not obtain a decisive role in managing the company. The union would probably be able to appoint at least one member to the company's board. Meanwhile, the U.S. government and Canadian and Ontario governments agreed to lend Chrysler billions of dollars to assist the company in its relaunch. Washington was to obtain an 8 per cent share of the company, in return for which the Treasury Department would select four independent directors. The Obama administration did not plan to play any direct role in managing the company.[14]

For its part, the Government of Canada agreed to contribute a loan of $2.5 billion to Chrysler, while Ontario would pony up $1.25 billion. Between them, Ottawa and Queen's Park would obtain a 2 per cent stake in the company and have one seat on the company's board. The restructured company was to have eight years to repay the Canadian loans.

The expectation was that as the government loans were paid off, Fiat's share in the company would rise eventually to a 35 per cent stake. Fiat's increased ownership would come in stages as it provided a distribution system for Chrysler vehicles outside North America, introduced a new fuel-efficient engine to be produced in Chrysler plants, and eventually built a Chrysler vehicle that would get forty miles per gallon.[15]

A month after the Chrysler bankruptcy, it was the turn of General Motors. By the time General Motors filed for bankruptcy on June 1, 2009, public opinion had been well prepared for the event. There was, however, no denying the historical significance of the event. More than any other company, the General Motors brand signified the twentieth-century industrial might of the United States. In 1953, when GM president Charles Wilson was nominated by President Dwight D. Eisenhower to serve as secretary of defense, Wilson was asked at a congressional hearing if he could conceive of ever having to take a decision that would run counter to the interests of General Motors. He replied that he could not, "because for years I thought what was good for the country was good for General Motors and vice versa."

The governments of the United States, Canada, and Ontario announced that they would put up a total of U.S.$60 billion to assist General Motors in re-establishing itself as a viable automaker. The Canadian share of this sum was U.S.$9.5 billion, with two-thirds of this amount coming from Ottawa and one-third from Queen's Park. The deal with GM, in return for the injection of the Canadian capital, was that the company would maintain 19 per cent of its combined Canada-U.S. production capacity in its Canadian plants. GM also undertook to invest in a new engine facility for its plant in St. Catharines, to invest $2.2 billion in its Canadian plants through 2016, and to put another $1 billion into research and development in Canada. By 2014 GM would employ only about 5,500 people in Canada. Under the arrangement, the federal and Ontario governments would obtain 12 per cent of the common shares of the relaunched company and about U.S.$1.7 billion in debt and preferred stock. The two governments would get to appoint one person to GM's thirteen-member board.[16]

One noteworthy aspect of the GM bankruptcy was the planned takeover of the company's European wing, Opel, by Canadian Frank Stronach, the chairman and controlling shareholder of Magna International, the giant auto-parts firm. In 2008 Opel produced and sold over 1.4 million vehicles in Europe. Its fleet includes sedans, compacts, minivans, and commercial vehicles. Several days before GM declared bankruptcy, Magna reached a tentative deal to invest $470 million (300 million euros) to acquire a 20 per cent stake in

Opel AG, Opel's largest operating unit in Europe, based in Germany. In a complicated deal involving the German government, Sherbank of Russia, GM itself, and Opel workers, as Stronach told *The Toronto Star*, "the industrial leadership" of the company would pass to Magna. Stronach stressed that his play for Opel could yield significant benefits to Canadians. He told the *Star* that he wanted Opel cars to be built in Canada.[17]

The Stronach venture aside, what are the implications of the role that Ottawa and Queen's Park are playing in the bailouts of Chrysler and General Motors? In an insightful article a couple of days after the GM bankruptcy, *Toronto Star* columnist Thomas Walkom pointed to what he called "a whiff of naïveté surrounding Canada's participation in the General Motors bailout." Walkom questioned whether "becoming a very junior partner in what's now Government Motors" will really provide effective support to Canada's auto industry. He said that under the deal, Ottawa and Queen's Park "are required to sell at least 30 per cent of their shares within three years, 65 per cent within six years and 100 per cent by 2018—regardless of the price they fetch." Meanwhile, the U.S. government is not required to do the same with its GM shares. Walkom made the case that the deal provided no job guarantees for Canada and that all the real power would be exercised south of the border. Was there any real alternative? Walkom suggested that there might have been another way:

> Germany, for instance, insisted that GM's Opel subsidiary in that country be excluded from any overall bankruptcy proceeding.
>
> Instead of putting money into the big GM pot, Germany focused on bailing out Opel. It even sought out new owners (including, ironically, Canadian Frank Stronach.)

Now, like GM, Opel has become a quasi-government firm. But at least Germans know that it's their government pulling the strings. Not someone else's.[18]

The predicament that Canada found itself in was not without precedent. In 1997, when it was faced with the need to reduce the scale of its operations, the French automaker Renault chose to shut down its assembly plant in Vilvoorde, Belgium. Tens of thousands of trade unionists from across Europe descended on Vilvoorde to protest the plant closing. Belgian workers concluded bitterly that they were the victims of a choice made by a foreign-owned auto company with very close connections to a foreign government.

After more than a century in the automotive industry, which became the country's most important manufacturing sector, Canada was failing to intervene effectively to safeguard jobs and plan coherently for the future. At every stage in the history of the Canadian auto industry, Canadian policy-making has been inadequate, never more than a house constructed on shifting sands. The branch-plant phase of the industry left it truncated, uncompetitive, and incapable of innovation. The Auto Pact reduced the Canadian auto industry to the position of a regional extension of another country's auto industry, a hostage to fortune.

With the onset of the FTA and NAFTA, Canada did what no other major auto-producing nation, with the exception of the United Kingdom, had ever done—it allowed its auto sector to slip almost entirely out of its effective jurisdiction. Ottawa and Queen's Park were reduced to supplicants who could cut taxes or throw money at auto companies, but little else. They were free, of course, to pray that their neo-liberal faith in the market was not misplaced.

Given the shabby record of the political parties on the issue of the auto industry and its future, auto workers, their families, and the inhabitants of the communities where the industry is vital could be forgiven for concluding that the country's political leadership has orphaned them.

And now, more briefly, we turn to trains and planes.

In both of these sectors, Canada has a storied past and plenty of strength in the present on which to build for the future. As in the case of the auto industry, the country has seen many failures and missteps, which should provide warnings for the future.

Nineteenth-century Canada was constructed around its railways. In the 1860s, one French-Canadian opponent of Confederation described Canada as a "railway in search of a country." The particular character of Canadian capitalism, the way the country was industrialized, the creation of the Canadian state, and the transcontinental expansion of the country were all intimately connected to railways. The first great Canadian railway, the Grand Trunk, which linked southern Ontario and southern Quebec, was in place by the time of Confederation. With many misadventures along the way, involving corruption at the highest levels, changes of government and corporate organization, the Canadian Pacific Railway was completed in the autumn of 1885, linking Canada from Montreal to Vancouver. The relationship between the Conservative government of John A. Macdonald and the CPR in the 1880s was so close that it was clear that the failure of either would mean catastrophe for the other. The Conservative government bestowed on the CPR $25 million in cash, twenty-five million acres of land along the right of way of the railway, huge tax breaks, and a twenty-year monopoly on the traffic of the West.

The railway linked the regions of the country together. It opened the door to the great age of the wheat economy, centred on the Prairies, and around it the sinews of a nation were constructed. All of this was done at an immense cost, however. The CPR and the major Canadian banks were enriched; the manufacturers of Central Canada were handed the captive market of the West as a consequence of both the railway and the high tariff that was the centrepiece of the National Policy; and the people of the Prairies were deeply alienated from the federal government, an instrument in their view of the powerful interests of the East, whose disproportionately high profits were wrung out of their labour on the farms.

The Canadian state remained centrally involved in the story of Canadian railways during the First World War, when the Conservative-Unionist governments of Robert Borden and Arthur Meighen nationalized two bankrupt railways to establish the publicly owned Canadian National Railways, the largest railway network in the country. The CNR, along with the privately owned CPR, remained at the centre of the Canadian transportation system for many decades, gradually succumbing in importance after the Second World War to the rise of highways and air travel. At the same time as airplanes, automobiles, and buses vastly reduced the role of rail in personal travel, railways were displaced to a very considerable extent in the shipping of goods by the rise of haulage by truck, and to a lesser extent the shipping of freight by air. During the 1990s, the Liberal government of Jean Chrétien privatized the CNR and undertook the privatization of Air Canada.

Now, in the early years of the twenty-first century, Canada's rail system is dilapidated and underfunded, a shadow of its glorious past. But now, too, with the threat of ever higher petroleum prices and the reality of peak oil, rail is being revisited in many countries as central to twenty-first-century transportation planning. When petroleum prices return to $150 a barrel, which they will, rail transport for both goods and people will become essential. Rail is more fuel-efficient, and the greenhouse gas emissions for rail per passenger per kilometre are a fraction of the emissions for automobiles and aircraft.[19] Still, despite romantic memories of the great days of Canadian rail, Canada is far behind other countries in realizing and contemplating what rail has to offer.

Canada faces two immense challenges on the subject of rail: the reconstruction of the national rail system so that it can handle a much larger proportion of freight haulage, as petroleum prices rise and the environmental costs of road use are addressed; and the need to construct dedicated high-speed rail systems to link major Canadian cities, along with the construction of tram and streetcar systems in the cities, and the expansion of urban subway systems.

To meet the first challenge Canada will have to rebuild and upgrade its railways, and in many cases lines will have to be twinned to make rail once again a mainstay in the haulage of freight. This absolutely necessary job will cost many billions of dollars. Only government can put up the capital for this gigantic venture, and it should only be undertaken in return for public-sector equity for the capital invested.

The second challenge has long been contemplated, and just as regularly governments have backed away from it—the construction of dedicated rail lines to carry travellers on high-speed trains between the cities in Canada where this is a viable proposition.

As is the case with freight, the passenger rail system is a remnant of its former self. In the heyday of passenger rail, both Canadian

National and Canadian Pacific operated their own routes, anchored on competing daily transcontinental trains that departed Montreal for Vancouver. Today, with the exception of special tourist trains in various parts of the country, passenger rail is largely run by Via Rail, a federal Crown corporation. Via Rail operates a transcontinental passenger service from Toronto to Vancouver and back a couple of times a week. While the train carries the proud name of the old CP service, "The Canadian," it runs on the CN line through northern Ontario and across the Prairies from Winnipeg through Saskatoon and Edmonton to Jasper and on to Vancouver. The glorious journey along the north shore of Lake Superior and from Winnipeg through Regina, Calgary, and Banff, en route to Vancouver, has been discontinued. All across the country, the story has been one of local and regional routes abandoned. Via Rail has made efforts to improve the speed and reliability of its service in Central Canada, but with limited success. The "fast" train from Toronto to Montreal takes four hours and forty-five minutes and is plagued with delays—it runs on lines dedicated first and foremost to freight.

One of the earliest policy-makers to consider the advantage of a light-rail system—not a high-speed system—to carry passengers from cities to towns and villages and to rural stops in between was Adam Beck, the manufacturer who turned Conservative politician and oversaw the creation of Ontario Hydro as a public utility. Beck believed that Ontario should construct a rail system, powered by Hydro's electricity, that went out from Toronto to cities, towns, villages, and rural stops in southern Ontario. He saw such a scheme, which did not come to fruition, as an alternative to automobiles in the region. That concept, which illustrates just how far-sighted Beck was, is now being realized in one form or another in many metropolitan areas and their peripheries around the world. The rail system in Sydney, Australia, for instance, ideally combines the role of a subway in the city itself and a commuter rail system linking the city to suburbs and towns and villages on the city's periphery. The San Francisco Bay Area Rapid Transit (BART) system is equivalent.

In the late twentieth century and in the first years of this century, a number of countries have developed high-speed passenger rail systems that effectively compete both with airlines and highways. They move people in speed and comfort with considerably greater energy efficiency than do competing modes of transport. Japan's bullet train system is one of the world's most advanced, with an average of 410,000 riders per day. So too is the French high-speed rail system—268,000 riders per day. The French Train à Grande Vitesse (TGV) network is operated by the SNCF, the publicly owned French rail operator. High-speed train systems are being constructed in many parts of the world, including Argentina, South Africa, and Saudi Arabia. They are being planned in Iran and Brazil. Even in the United States, long a laggard when it comes to passenger rail, billions of dollars are being spent to extend high-speed rail outside the Boston-Washington corridor, and plans are in the works for a high-speed link between San Francisco and Los Angeles.[20]

In France the first TGV service opened between Paris and Lyon in 1981. Today a journey between the two cities takes two hours, and you can set your watch by the departures and arrivals. High-toned Parisians even take the TGV to Lyon for lunch in one of the city's fine restaurants—Lyon is regarded by many as the food capital of the world—and then return in the afternoon. The TGV system has now been developed all across France, with lines built as a series of spokes from Paris to other cities. Today the fastest TGV service between two cities averages just under 280 kilometres an hour. A TGV test run set the record for the fastest wheeled train at 574.8 kilometres an hour. The French system has been extended to other countries, including Belgium, Germany, and Spain, and goes through the Channel Tunnel to London.

The TGV system has changed France. Commuters who work in Paris now live in cities such as Tours on the Loire, from whence they can be in the capital and on their way to their offices in an hour. The TGV very effectively competes with air travel between French cities, and it competes as well with automobile travel.

The distance from Paris to Lyon is a little less than the distance from Toronto to Montreal. Imagine the benefits of a train that runs on time, delivering passengers in two hours from one downtown to the other of Canada's two largest cities. Consider, as well, the consequences. Such a train system would effectively compete both with airlines and automobiles. Centred in Quebec, Bombardier already manufactures high-speed trains and is perfectly capable of producing the trains that would be required for a Canadian network. A high-speed train system running from Windsor to Quebec City with lines to Ottawa would serve more than half the population of Canada. A line from Edmonton to Calgary would serve two of the country's major metropolises. Another line could be feasible from Halifax to Moncton.

The billions of dollars needed to establish these high-speed train systems would have to come from government. The investment in the future of Canadian cities and industry and the contribution to the country's effort to reduce greenhouse gas emissions would be immense. As in the case of the auto industry, no leadership has come forth from the federal or provincial levels for such projects. The Harper government and the Liberal opposition are far too tied into the neo-liberal approach to the economy to do anything on the large scale about all of this. And so, although the potential exists, there is no leadership to make rail what it needs to be in twenty-first-century Canada.

———————

As in the cases of autos and rail, aircraft manufacturing in Canada has been a tale of stunning successes and enormous failures.

Just as the development of Southern Canada is linked in reality and in the imagination to railways, the push to the North is indelibly connected with the stories of bush pilots and the sturdy planes they flew into the tundra. The Chipmunk, Caribou, Otter, Beaver, and other planes manufactured by the de Havilland Aircraft Company were flown by the solitary figures who became legendary in the North.

In the populous South, the history of aviation was less romantic, but the record was inspiring nonetheless. Beginning in late 1937, Canadians rose to the challenge under the leadership of the federal government and established Trans-Canada Airlines, the Crown corporation that was the predecessor to Air Canada.

The record of Canadians in the creation of revolutionary new aircraft in the postwar years combined both inspirational highs and crushing lows. In 1949 the world's first jet passenger airliner was developed in Canada. Technically ahead of its competitors, the aircraft failed for a reason that would bedevil other Canadian breakthroughs. Corporations and states in other countries were determined to stand behind their own products and the economic development they promised, leaving the Jetliner and its successors out in the cold.

Then came the Avro Arrow, the development by Canadian designers, engineers, and workers of the finest jet fighter in the world at the end of the 1950s. On a black day in 1959 the Diefenbaker government pulled the plug on the magnificent aircraft, concluding that there would be an insufficient foreign market for the Arrow and that Canada could not sustain the production of the plane on its own. Thousands of Canadians, highly skilled in every aspect of the development and production of aircraft, lost their jobs. Many of these left the country to work in the aircraft industry in California and for the National Aeronautics and Space Administration (NASA) in Texas and Florida. The aircraft industry in Ontario never recovered from the blow dealt by the demise of the Arrow. The Canadian state, during and after the Second World War, underwrote and bankrolled the rise of A.V. Roe, the company that created the Arrow. Then Ottawa let the industry die.

The next successful chapter in the history of the Canadian aircraft industry was fostered by the state capitalism of the government of Quebec. The single greatest success story of Quebec's new entrepreneurialism was Bombardier, the company that used its development of, and huge market for, snowmobiles as the launch pad for the development and production of trains and planes. At present Bombardier is gambling heavily on its launch of a new series of regional jets, and is being backed with interest-free loans from both the federal and Quebec governments. With many airlines around the world facing bankruptcy and with high-speed trains emerging as a more fuel-efficient alternative to regional jets, this is indeed a high stakes venture.

As in the cases of trains and trams, the presence of Bombardier could hold the key to a successful domestic adaptation to the challenges of Canadian aviation in an era of high energy prices and the need to reduce greenhouse gas emissions.

———————

All of Canada's transportation equipment sectors—auto, rail, and aircraft—have seen inspiring successes and deplorable failures. In the future, if we are to establish economically and environmentally viable auto, rail, and aircraft industries in Canada, two principles, so regularly ignored in the past, need to be front and centre: paying attention to the interests of those who work in the industries and the communities in which they live; and the necessity of Canadian control.

Nothing stands in the way of Canadians using their capital, resources, and skills to tackle these multiple challenges and to create industries for the twenty-first century—nothing, that is, except for the ideas of a failed ideology.

President Obama is certainly correct when he says that a new, green fleet of automobiles, and indeed trains, trams, subways, and aircraft, will need to be constructed for the twenty-first century. That fact has already registered all around the world. In Asia, Europe, and the United States, companies and unions in partnership with governments will be working out plans to design and build these vehicles. Everyone knows that the countries, companies, and workforces that seize the high ground in the creation of these vehicles will be placed to do well in the industrial competition of coming decades. So far, Canadians have barely begun to think about all of this. The reason is simple enough. Governments, political leaders, and industrial communities are still thinking in terms of the major U.S. auto companies doing most of that job in Canada.

To count on these corporations would be to make an error of historic proportions. A variety of geostrategic circumstances, having to do with the decline of the British Empire and the rise of its U.S. successor, allowed Canada to become the site of a large-scale auto industry even though the companies that assembled vehicles in Canada were based in the United States and Asia. It will require enormous pools of capital to cope with the start-up costs to conceive and manufacture green vehicles for the twenty-first century. Canada has the capital. What it lacks at the political, governmental, and corporate levels is the boldness and the imagination to think outside the twentieth-century branch-plant box in which we remain cloistered. We have not much time to break out and chart a new course.

There is an alternative to placing our faith in the share of production that we can glean on our side of the border from the next generation of U.S. or Japanese automakers, or the Fiats of the world who arrive in the guise of a knight to the rescue, but intend to use our present misfortune to gouge our workers and communities. The alternative is to design and build cars and trucks in Canada for Canadians and for export. Such a grand project will require the ingenuity, imagination, and boldness that we lacked in the last century. We have the expertise, the workforce, and plenty of experience in designing virtually all aspects of auto production from batteries to power electric vehicles to engines and subassemblies.

What makes this a moment of immense opportunity for those who will seize it is that all of the vehicle manufacturers in the world are starting from scratch, just as their predecessors were at the beginning of the twentieth century. The internal combustion engine, propelled by gasoline, transformed the world's cities and the lives of billions of people. For the working people who built them and for the wage and salary earners who drove them, automobiles delivered mobility and freedom that the wealthiest people of a few generations earlier would have found unimaginable.

But the automobile in a time of global warming, peak oil, and choking cities now threatens the people of the world. Once a liberator, in its present form it imprisons. This fundamental condition of our new century is understood all around the world. We are starting from scratch in the creation of the new personal vehicles—call them cars—that must be conceived alongside the other transportation modes of our time. We are starting from scratch with ideas for how to re-create our cities, shift from petroleum to other fuels, and sharply reduce the emission of greenhouse gases.

As in the case of automobiles, we need to act on constructing high-speed train systems. In February 2009 the Ontario and Quebec governments announced that they would be spending $3 million to study the viability of a high-speed train network in the Windsor to Quebec City corridor. There is nothing wrong with that, except that since 1973 there have been sixteen previous studies or plans to study such a scheme. One study conducted in 1995 concluded that a high-speed rail system in the corridor would cost $18.3 billion. Accounting for inflation, that would now amount to $23.9 billion.[21] The price tag is large, but alongside the price tag for highways and airports and linkages to airports, it becomes not just reasonable, but essential. Not only will the capital cost of the system pay for itself in several decades, but the benefits of more energy-efficient travel in the country's most populous region will also be enormous—and will contribute to urban development all along the line.

The reconstruction of our transportation equipment industries is central to the rebuilding of our cities and to the relaunching of our economy for a new global economy. Holding us back from entering the coming global economy on advantageous terms and seeking to play a crucial role in it is our habit of dependence. In addition, of course, there is our colonial-minded business class whose members still believe in the discredited shibboleths of neo-liberalism. Then too is the matter of governments that have not the faintest idea of the existing opportunities.

We need a new model to plan a wide range of Canadian initiatives. The federal government, the provinces, and the cities must be involved in this project. The private sector, trade unions, and the best brains in a range of fields must be brought on board.

Because we are considering something entirely new, the model for managing these new enterprises should also abandon past practices. Instead of the top-down workplace models of the twentieth century, where creativity was left at the door when wage and salary earners entered, we can use this sector as the proving ground for industrial democracy and worker input and decision-making. These concepts have been much talked about over the past two centuries, and sometimes tried. We can push them further.

Chapter Thirteen

A PROGRESSIVE ECONOMIC

STRATEGY FOR CANADA

_____

NOW I NEED to shift the tone of the narrative from the analytical to the aspirational. In fact, the analytical and the aspirational are aspects of the same underlying motivation: to comprehend the world and to change it for the better. Analysis itself is conducted out of the desire to understand, not for its own sake, but to comprehend so as to make possible fruitful changes. The aspirational, in a similar vein, does not spring forth as a mental product alone, but is deeply influenced by how things actually are and therefore could be.

In Western cultures, the development of new and ever more effective techniques is always a central starting point.

If, for instance, I advance the argument that we as Canadians need a new economic strategy to achieve societal goals different from those pursued with a previous strategy, the reply will be: yes, but can it work? We are, on the surface at least, oriented in our thinking towards techniques, technology, and the pursuit of the workable rather than the pursuit of the ideal. Fair enough. If that is our starting point, my assertion is that neo-liberalism has failed. Its techniques have been exposed as utterly inadequate. But let me take this a step further. Neo-liberalism has not merely delivered a failed set of techniques for managing the economy. It is in itself, as well, to borrow a phrase, a god that has failed, an ideology constructed to advance the interests of capitalists, of those who control capital, as the supposedly vital centre of our civilization whose pursuits should be privileged ahead of all others.

This is a moment for pause. If, as I have argued in these pages, the techniques of neo-liberalism have failed, and its goals have been exposed as a dead end for humanity, we are required to advance the arguments in favour of the use of different techniques for the purpose of pursuing a different set of goals.

The case I will make here is based on the desirability of establishing a Canadian economic strategy that privileges the whole of the Canadian population rather than those who have controlled capital under the neo-liberal model. Such a model begins necessarily by asserting that it is labour in all its forms that creates capital and not, as neo-liberalism insists, that capital is the source of wealth.

A couple of operating principles ought to underpin the model. An operating principle needs to be workable, and it has to be focused on a central objective: in this case, the reconstruction of the Canadian economy to serve the interests of the broad majority of Canadians. First, the investment by government to bail out particular companies or sectors of the economy should only be made in return for public equity in the company or sector. Second, the Canadian economy ought to be reconstructed to be both more Canadian and more international in its orientation. The overwhelmingly continental orientation of recent decades has been too restrictive in blocking Canadian initiatives, and it shuts out the wider world beyond the United States to too great a degree.

The question underlying the first operating principle—on whose behalf should government expenditures be undertaken?— has become crucial in a time of multi-billion-dollar bailouts for banks and auto companies, among others. The population of the world has been living through a gigantic teach-in on the subject of what the capitalists and their governments do when major financial institutions and other huge corporations get into trouble. Governments all over the world have spent trillions of dollars to bail out banks and automobile companies. What the people of the world have learned is that when things go seriously wrong for major corporations, a time out is called and all the rules by which we supposedly live are suspended. Governments that are purportedly devoted to free enterprise, a system in which companies rise or fall by how they perform in the marketplace, stop the game and engage in the greatest investment of public capital ever undertaken in the history of the world. The public money spent since the autumn of 2008 to save capitalism from its own excesses has left all public-sector investments, with the exception of military spending, undertaken over the past century exposed as a mere pittance.

In Canada the federal and Ontario governments have invested billions of dollars to keep General Motors and Chrysler in business. With much less fanfare, the federal government has come to the aid of the country's banks on an enormous scale. In autumn 2008 the Harper government undertook a $75-billion bailout on behalf of the country's chartered banks. Because there were no bank failures in Canada and because Prime Minister Harper insisted that the government's aid to the banks was not a bailout— "This is not a bailout; this is a market transaction that will cost the government nothing," he declared on October 10—the move generated little media analysis. Finance Minister Flaherty added, "This program is an efficient, cost-effective and safe way to support lending in Canada that comes at no fiscal cost to taxpayers."[1]

Compared to what was happening south of the border, the Canadian action was made to seem entirely innocuous. What occurred, however, was indeed a massive bailout that has cost the taxpayers a huge sum of money. The bailout began four days prior to the October federal election with the announcement that the Canada Mortgage and Housing Corporation (CMHC), a federal government institution, would buy up to $25 billion in mortgages in order to support the country's credit market. The purchases of the mortgages pumped money into the banks that they could use in any way that they liked. Among the ways in which the banks could use the money was by purchasing government bonds that would allow them to earn a profit from the deficit that the government was running, in part to keep the banks healthy.

The first tranche of $25 billion was followed by the announcement of a further $50 billion on November 12, 2008. The official announcement of the $50 billion included the following rationale: "The Honourable Jim Flaherty, Minister of Finance, today announced the Government will purchase up to an additional $50 billion of insured mortgage pools by the end of the fiscal year as part of its ongoing efforts to maintain the availability of longer-term credit in Canada."[2]

The government's claim that providing $75 billion for the banks involved no outlay on the part of taxpayers was made on the theory that what was involved was simply a swap. The government was providing the capital in return for the mortgages, which were not toxic mortgages, but securities worth as much as the money the banks were getting. First of all, in a market in which housing values were falling, this was a fatuous claim. In a market in which property values were rising, the banks would have regarded the government's move as an expropriation of valuable assets. Moreover, the government announced that it would sell government bonds and other financial instruments to raise the money to undertake the purchase of the mortgages, thereby effectively adding to Ottawa's indebtedness.

What Ottawa was doing was transferring a vast pool of capital, equivalent to nearly 5 per cent of the country's Gross Domestic Product, to the banks. A bailout, this was, and a gigantic one at that. South of the border, when Washington pumped hundreds of billions of dollars into U.S. banks (the Canadian injection, relative to the size of the Canadian economy compared to the U.S. economy, was equivalent to about $600 billion in U.S. terms) under the Troubled Assets Relief Program, an explosive public debate took place in Congress and in the mainstream media. On the progressive side of the U.S. political spectrum, including people such as Paul Krugman, the Nobel Prize–winning economist and *New York Times* columnist, the case was made for the nationalization of the banks. If the public was putting up the cash, Krugman and others reasoned, the public should acquire voting shares in the banks for the risk being taken. In Canada, there was scarcely a peep. Canadian banks were being recapitalized, made more powerful and profitable through an enormous injection of public capital, and scarcely anyone noticed.

In the eyes of the government, the Canadian banks were much too big to be allowed to fail, and the bankers who ran them much too important to permit anything to interfere with the remuneration they took home. Retired auto workers were an entirely different matter, however. In April 2009, Ontario premier Dalton McGuinty said the province would not bail out the fund that guaranteed the pensions of retired General Motors workers in the event that the company sought bankruptcy protection, which could imperil the pensions received by retired GM workers. The premier explained that the province could not afford to top up Ontario's $100-million Pension Benefits Guarantee Fund, a fund set up to aid pensioners when company pension plans go broke, in the event of GM going bankrupt.

"It's certainly not our intention to put more money into the Pension Benefits Guarantee Fund," McGuinty said. "We need to be fair to all Ontario seniors and if we look to those without pensions to restore vitality to pensions for those who benefit from those pensions, I don't think that's fair." The premier added that the province had provided billions of dollars in aid to the auto companies and that using taxpayer money to guarantee auto-worker pensions when 65 per cent of Ontarians had no pension plan would be a tough sell.[3]

Consider the thinking here. For the province to pump billions of dollars into the auto companies to keep them, their shareholders, and their managements afloat was a reasonable thing to do. On the other hand, to assist retired auto workers in the event that their pensions were cut off, through no fault of their own, was something that could not be contemplated. The workers we are speaking of had worked on the assembly line at GM for thirty years with the expectation that when they retired they would receive the pension that had been negotiated for them by their union with the company. When the crash occurred, these retirees, who were in no position to return to work, faced the prospect that their incomes could be cut off. While the McGuinty government was prepared to provide vast sums of money to the auto companies when the crash occurred, it was not ready to do any such thing for the retired auto workers.

Instead, what the government of Ontario did was to put the onus for the survival of the pensions on the CAW, insisting that if the union made sufficient concessions to the company, GM could be kept alive and so too would the pensions. The Ontario government strategy dovetailed with that of the federal government. Between them, Queen's Park and Ottawa relentlessly pressured the CAW to make concessions to GM. The alternative was the bankruptcy of the company, which would leave the workers and the retirees in an even more desperate situation.

Right before the eyes of Canadians was a demonstration that their governments were prepared to do whatever it took to keep banks and auto companies afloat—violating all the shibboleths of free enterprise in the process, while hanging out the workers to dry.

———————

A progressive economic policy for Canada must begin by reversing these completely unacceptable priorities—by putting the people of Canada first, and reducing the companies to the role of serving the needs of the people. Capital needs to become the servant of the people, not the other way around. The capital accumulated as a consequence of the labour of Canadians needs to be invested to benefit them.

That is a radical idea, but an entirely reasonable one. When ideas for sweeping change come from the progressive side of the political spectrum, they are ridiculed as impractical or too expensive. That ridicule is much harder to carry off today than it was prior to the autumn of 2008. It is now completely clear to what lengths governments will go in bailing out companies.

In my opinion, every nickel of public revenue invested to aid financial institutions, the auto industry, or any other sector of the economy should be in return for voting shares in the companies aided. This is not an unknown concept in Canada. During the First World War, public funds were invested to salvage two bankrupt railways in Canada by nationalizing the companies and bringing them under the ownership of the federal government as the Canadian National Railways. A century ago the Ontario government concluded that for Ontario manufacturing to be competitive with U.S. manufacturing, the province required a cheap, reliable source of electric power. To meet this goal, the province set up Ontario Hydro as a Crown corporation, taking over the privately owned power companies in the process. Publicly owned companies have been used in many sectors of the economy when needed. Today, as governments are spending more than ever before in history to aid ailing sectors of the economy, Canada should go the route of Crown ownership, used so often and successfully in the past. So that the capital that Canadians create through their labour serves them, investments of public capital need to result in Crown ownership and control.

On the second operating principle, it is time for Canadians to rethink their economic position in the world.

Over the course of their history, Canadians have lived under the sway of three empires: the French, British, and American. In each case, as they shifted from one empire to the next, once by conquest and the second time by circumstance and to some extent by choice, Canadians ended up being associated with the leading power of the day. It could be comforting to believe that Canadian elites were making clever choices, choosing to desert one empire for another at just the right time; but nothing of the kind was happening. Canadian elites, not least today, have been very slow to strike out on their own and to make a choice for their country and themselves that involves cutting their ties with the dominant foreign power of the day. This is not surprising. Elite status in Canada, for the most part, has been bestowed on those who knew how to make the best of things within a dependent country whose economy and strategic interests were closely tied to those of another, much bigger power.

Now, once again, as was the case with the declining British Empire a century ago, Canadians are living through a time when they are tied to a declining power. While the United States will remain enormously influential in the world, it will not be the global colossus it has been for more than sixty years. What does that mean for Canada?

As the crash struck Canada, the first response of Canadian politicians was to deny it or to blame each other in less than insightful ways for its consequences. The more enduring response, on the part of the Harper government, the Ignatieff Liberals, and to a considerable extent the NDP and the Bloc Québécois, has been to count on a U.S. economic recovery to generate recovery in Canada. The nation's political and economic leaders are banking on the resumption of the status quo ante. Canada, they believe, will return to the role of an exporter of commodities, overwhelmingly to the United States. It will be a country that also does some manufacturing in sectors such as the automotive industry, largely under the auspices of foreign-owned multinationals.

Harper and Ignatieff focus on little beyond how the economic crisis will play out to benefit or to harm their political fortunes. Neither they and their parties nor, to be fair to them, the leaders of the other parties have done any serious thinking about how the global geopolitical system is at a parting of the ways: the end of one age and the beginning of another.

Has it occurred to them that wagering Canada's future almost entirely on a declining, deeply indebted United States, whose living standard is almost certain to fall, may not be the wisest choice? Not at all. Look at the embarrassingly dependent course they pursued on the auto industry.

The country's political leaders do not think in large terms because they have rarely had to. Nor does the utterly unimaginative, supine Canadian corporate elite. Those who run the nation's large corporations, whether the companies are foreign or domestically owned, with a few notable exceptions (a Frank Stronach here, a Jim Balsillie there), did not get where they are because they think, but because they are so utterly conventional. Add to the list the country's second-rate mainstream media, with its derivative right-wing private newspapers and television networks and the fearful CBC, and you have few wide-ranging explorations of alternative visions for the country's future in the public realm as well.

Is all of this reason for gloom among Canadians? Not in my opinion.

Canadians are a well-educated, productive people with a deep commitment to their country. They have all the means they require to strike out on a socio-economic course of their own in the twenty-first century, a course broadly congruent with global developments. What I am talking about is not autarchy, but an engagement with the outside world that is more on our own terms than has been the case in the past. And by the outside world, I do not mean the United States to the virtual exclusion of all else.

Consider this: until the mid-1920s Canada did more trade with Britain than with the United States. Today, just under 80 per cent of Canada's exports are destined for the United States. That is a higher proportion than in the years immediately following the Second World War, when the United States accounted for nearly 50 per cent of global economic output, compared to just over 20 per cent today. The plain fact is that Canada has focused its exports ever more on the United States at the same time as the U.S. share of global economic output has declined. Canada's trading relationship with the outside world is more continental, and less global, than it was a century ago.

That pattern has to be broken if Canada is to be successful in the twenty-first century. And along with that shift, Canadians also need to break out of the straitjacket of the NAFTA rules, and they have to gain control of the major pools of capital that their economy generates. These are the necessary pillars of a new Canadian economic strategy.

Problems will only continue to mount if Canada does not adopt such an approach. Unless Canada strikes out to fashion its own place in the new global economy, it will end up as a series of slowly declining regions tacked onto the northern perimeter of the United States. If that seems to be an unreasonable proposition, consider how a hundred years ago analysts might have argued that it was not in Canada's interest to remain as attached to Britain as it was at the time—and how such a proposition stated in the early years of the twentieth century would have drawn scorn and disbelief from the conventional powers-that-be.

Canadians have a choice. They can continue with political leaders content to carry on with the present arrangements, but such a choice, taken with a shrug of the shoulder, will lead to the country doing less well in this century than it did in the last.

The more active choice, made as a consequence of thought and political mobilization, is more difficult, but it alone will allow the people of Canada to make of themselves what they are capable of in this century. Many peoples will be striving to prepare themselves for the economic recovery to come. Canadians will need a new political and economic leadership to make that journey towards an economic strategy that will work for them. They will need a strategy that is a just one for the majority of Canadians and not simply for the few who benefit from neo-liberalism.

Using public funds to relaunch key sectors of the economy, and in the process acquiring Crown ownership or control, will open the door to the establishment of a position in the global economy that extends far beyond our almost exclusive ties with the United States. To achieve such a reorientation, Canada will need to put a stop to two restrictive elements of NAFTA: the provision that Canada has to supply the United States with petroleum on an ongoing basis and that it cannot establish price controls for the domestic sale of petroleum while exporting oil and natural gas at the world price; and the National Treatment provision of the trade agreement, which prevents Canada from choosing key sectors in which domestic firms can be promoted as centres of excellence based on exports of manufactured products and not simply commodities. The National Treatment provision requires Canada to treat U.S. firms on the same basis as Canadian firms, thereby blocking the establishment of any viable sort of planned economic strategy. With neo-liberalism in tatters, Canadians should not be forced to live under the restraints of neo-liberalism in a world in which others, certainly not the Americans, are not going to play by these rules. To rid Canada of these unacceptable constraints, the government should attempt to renegotiate NAFTA with the United States and Mexico to alter the rules under which the member countries operate. If that effort should fail, Canada should announce that it will leave NAFTA, under the terms spelled out in the agreement.

In today's world, the tried-and-not-so-true approaches have become the path of recklessness. If Canadians decide that they are going to strike out on an innovative course to cope with a new global economy, they are free to do so. All that stands in our way are failed leaders and their failed policies.

Chapter Fourteen

ECONOMICS FOR HUMANITY

———————

ASK NOT FOR WHOM the bell tolls. It tolls the din of imploding financial institutions, crashing stocks, choked credit markets, and government bailouts. It tolls the end of an age. What is to come may be better, it may be worse. It will be different.

What has ended is the Anglo-American era of globalization, with its ever vaster financial markets, deregulation, and the out-sourcing of production to the cheapest available pools of labour. At the helm were the members of a ruling class nourished on bonuses, mergers, and acquisitions, people who never spared a thought for those whose lives they were blithely reordering, often destroying.

The deeply entrenched myths of neo-liberalism have been suffering the death of a thousand cuts. Edward Liddy, the chief executive of the American International Group, appointed for one dollar a year to clean up the mess after the U.S. federal government acquired an 80 per cent share in the company in the fall of 2008, continued to cling to one of the most cherished of the myths: the need to pay fabulous sums to retain topnotch business talent. In March 2009 the news broke that following the receipt of additional bailout funds from Washington, AIG had paid out bonuses to 418 employees; the bonuses, totalling U.S.\$165 million, included more than \$1 million each to 73 people. The result was a wave of popular fury that swept across the United States. Although the Obama administration had not designed the bailout package and was simply paying out funds put in place by the previous Bush administration, the new president felt the heat from the American people.

Just as the news of the bonuses broke, Liddy presented the time-honoured rationale for such payments: "We cannot attract and retain the best and brightest talent to lead and staff the AIG businesses—which are now being operated principally on behalf of American taxpayers—if employees believe their compensation is subject to continued and arbitrary adjustment by the U.S. Treasury."[1]

Andrew Cuomo, the attorney general of New York State—who was trying to find a way of clawing back the bonuses—dismissed Liddy's defence of the "best and brightest": "Their mythology starts with the false premise that these are irreplaceable geniuses."[2]

The myth of the best and brightest, in one form or another, has served to justify the practices of U.S. capitalism, particularly the vast inequality of the rewards system, for the past two centuries. At the heart of the myth is the idea that liberty tied tightly to inequality is the key to economic success. Only by holding out the lure of enormous monetary gains can those with the potential to become truly gifted entrepreneurial giants be nurtured to their full potential. Americans like to contrast their system with two other kinds of systems—those based too much on inherited wealth, and those based too much on the idea of income equality. The first system, that of inherited wealth, Americans associated with the Europeans and their aristocracies. The second, that of stultifying equality, they associated with all forms of socialism or social democracy, not to mention communism. Some two centuries ago the American story of the poor, hard-working boy who made good was repeatedly told in the writings of a New England author named Horatio Alger.

The Horatio Alger myth does not hold up well when the harsh light of facts is shone on it. For one thing, inheritance has played a much bigger role in shaping the U.S. capitalist class than the cheer-leaders for the American variety of capitalism like to admit. Social mobility in the United States has been no greater than in Western Europe, Canada, or Australia. Indeed, the U.S. capitalist system has always placed immense obstacles in the path of advancement for African Americans and Hispanics; and social mobility for women has been no greater in the United States than in other Western countries.

Myths die hard, though. To a much greater extent than is the case in other countries, American history has been replete with the celebration of corporate titans—from John D. Rockefeller to Bill Gates and Warren Buffett. In recent years, while Bill Gates remains an illustrious figure, the reputation of Buffett, known as the Oracle of Omaha, has reached proportions usually reserved for kings or Roman emperors. Buffett's corporate holding company, Berkshire Hathaway, is closely watched by the business media and by the pub-lic at large. Prior to the crash in the autumn of 2008, investors in Berkshire Hathaway tended to revere Buffett as a financial genius who spoke the language of plain common sense. One way the crash made Buffett appear all too human flowed from his ownership of a 20 per cent share of Moody's Corporation, the parent company of Moody's Investors Service, a firm that rates investments and grades the debt issued by corporations and financial institutions. As it turned out, Moody's, along with other ratings agencies, gave positive ratings to a long list of sub-prime mortgage-related securities that are now generally seen as toxic. Moody's bestowed an A2 rating on Lehman Brothers just days before the company filed for bankruptcy. In addition, Moody's gave the unsecured debt of AIG an even higher A2 rating immediately prior to Washington's bailout of the insurance giant. That bailout ultimately amounted to U.S.$170 billion.

In his annual Berkshire Hathaway letter in March 2009, sent to the company's investors, Buffett, usually noted for his frankness and willingness to engage in self-criticism, said nothing about Moody's shocking performance. He may have been preoccupied by Berkshire Hathaway's own record. The conglomerate suffered its worst year ever, with its net income falling 96 per cent in the fourth quarter of 2008.[3]

A simple error that leads to endless confusion about the global economic crisis has to do with what is the real foundation of the economy. Capitalists, neo-classical economists, and those unfortunate enough to have studied economics or to have attended a business school believe that capital is the foundation of the economy. They are flat wrong.

The underlying idea of the financial system that crashed is that the investment of capital is the thing that creates wealth. Beginning with the neo-conservative revolution at the end of the 1970s in Britain and the United States, deregulating capital so that it could flow anywhere without restriction has been understood as the key to unleashing the market forces that will make the economy grow. Let investment travel to all parts of the world, allow businesses to acquire one another, and remove remaining protective trade barriers, and a better world will be established, in developing countries and developed countries alike. In this chemistry of globalization, utopianism and greed were bound together. This revolution—most accurately depicted as neo-liberalism, although it was unleashed by neo-conservatives—realized the dreams of capitalists as never before. The nation-state, mobilized during the postwar decades to cater to labour as the junior partner of capital in the advanced countries, was tamed to put mobility of capital ahead of all else. Deregulation and technological revolution combined to free capitalism not only from trade unions and the state, but also from the restraints of time. Capital could be transferred at the flick of a cursor from anywhere to anywhere. Virtual transfers of capital quickly dwarfed commerce in commodities. Markets never closed.

Be careful what you wish for. Utopia unleashed became dystopia achieved. The world made safe for investors became a world in which workers were exploited on an unprecedented scale, cities mushroomed into barrios for the dispossessed, the impoverished braved the seas in their quest for jobs and survival, and environmental catastrophe loomed. In the end, neo-liberalism wrought its own self-destruction, much in the same way as Soviet communism had a couple of decades earlier.

In the economically advanced countries, those who run the dominant corporations, lead the major political parties, and set the agenda for business schools, economics departments, and pro-business think tanks aspire to the reconstruction of the neo-liberal order. That is not to say that these people, representing quite different organizations, and nurtured in diverse national cultures, do not hold a wide range of views about what ought to be done. It is not unfair, however, to ascribe to the overwhelming majority of these people the broad desire to remake the world to be essentially the way it was on the eve of the crash. This assertion is not rendered invalid because many people in the economic and political elites want to reform and reregulate financial systems and fiscal arrangements to avoid sub-prime housing meltdowns, the collapse of financial institutions, and the dangerous consequences of various forms of indebtedness. What they do want, in general, is to restore capitalism to health to allow its pre-crash system of rewards to prevail.

———————

Now what? Should humanity mobilize its political, economic, and societal skills to painstakingly reconstruct the system that has crashed? That is certainly the goal of the Obama administration, the Brown government in the United Kingdom, the Harper government in Ottawa (to the extent that it has any understanding of what is happening), and other governments in the West. Even if Obama understands that the financial sector in the United States had grown too large and must be cut back in size as the U.S. economy recovers, it is nonetheless his intention to re-create U.S. and global capitalism with its rewards and its priorities essentially unaltered.

What we have, though, is a historic opportunity for people around the world with entirely different aspirations to come to the fore. During the neo-liberal era, the hegemonic power of the ruling ideas pushed to the margins alternative conceptions about how to order the economy.

In comparison to the postwar era, when a comparatively wide range of socio-economic options were being broadly advocated and considered, the past three decades have been a time of ever narrower legitimate options. It has been the age of TINA—there is no alternative—an age of reaction during which the concept of citizenship has been eroded, the social state has been substantially dismantled, and those who control capital have been empowered as never before in all of human history.

That is not to say that during this time progressives did not fight large battles. They even won some of them. Most significant have been the struggles for the environment, gay and lesbian rights, anti-racism, and the rights and aspirations of women, in particular their reproductive rights.

The long retreat of the past thirty years has been on the terrain of the collective power and rights of working people all over the world, from the best-paid salary earners in the advanced countries to the super-exploited wage earners in the garment factories in the poor countries. As organized labour has been thrown on the defensive and social and educational programs have been rolled back, the power of capital has grown ever more complete. The extent of the retreat is captured in the increasing reliance on the philanthropy of the rich and the super-rich in a wide range of fields.

A contradictory outlook faces wage and salary earners throughout the world today. On the one hand, the savage economic downturn and the loss of many millions of jobs around the globe have reduced the bargaining power of labour still further. Highly visible has been the massive political and corporate pressure on unionized Canadian and U.S. auto workers to accept enormous cuts to their overall remuneration, in the form of reduced pay and benefits to those still working and slashed payouts to retirees. Similar pressures have been applied to workers around the world to force them to make do with lower wages and less generous benefits. The existence of a gigantic reserve army of unemployed workers strengthens the government and corporate assault on wage and salary earners.

Yet the neo-liberal system worldwide has visibly failed, with the top corporate managers being reduced in the eyes of humanity from demi-gods to greedy incompetents. Never in history were the rulers of the economic system so humiliated as in 2008–9. It is not that their predecessors during the Great Depression of the 1930s were not scathingly and brilliantly castigated. The difference is that in the age of twenty-four-hour cable news and the Internet, the spotlight on those who have made government and corporate decisions has become unceasing.

Populist anger against financiers has boiled to the surface, not only in the United States, but in many countries. Members of the general public no longer believe the words of those who direct, or formerly directed, major financial institutions—much less those at the helm of governments, although some leaders have more credibility than others. The low esteem in which those who steer the economy are now held has opened the door to new ideas, or the restatement of old ideas, from across the political spectrum.

On the political right in the United States, Republicans have been returning to the political verities that constituted their stock in trade before the crash. Rather than facing up to the role of their policies in generating the economic catastrophe, with few exceptions the Republicans are promoting their belief in small government and tax cuts. On the face of it, this may seem a short-sighted, even foolish, political strategy, and perhaps events and the passage of time will prove that it is. If Obama's policies prove effective in combating the economic crisis, or are understood by the U.S. public as having been effective, the Republicans will end up as the great political losers out of all of this. On the other hand, if the economic crisis is protracted and the activism and fiscal stimulus of the Obama administration do not restore the United States to economic health, and if a wide swath of the U.S. public draws the conclusion that conditions were better before Obama took power, things could turn out very differently.

Obama's centrist policies, aimed at restoring U.S. capitalism, by and large, to the way things were before the crash, may well be deemed a failure. In that case the door will be opened not only to the ideas of the Republican Party, but to all manner of populist demagoguery on the far right. The conditions that face us are similar to those of the 1930s in one very important respect. When centrist politicians and their policies do not succeed in mitigating the desperate economic plight of millions of people, powerful authoritarian movements spring up to grapple with the anxieties of the age with programs that are the very antithesis of democracy. In the 1930s the fascists and Nazis filled the void when mainstream democrats dithered and failed to come to grips with urgent problems such as mass unemployment and poverty. The solutions of the authoritarians can involve not merely the elimination of democratic rights, but the imprisonment of thousands, and in the most extreme cases the murder of millions.

———————

In a book that warns of the danger to democracy itself as a consequence of the crash, long-time French politician and writer Jacques Attali concludes that the choices before humanity are stark indeed.[4] A progressive alternative is urgently needed. It will have to be an alternative that will not cloak the current crisis in exclusionism, racism, and anti-immigrant sentiment, the desperate remedies that always are on offer from the far right. The vigour of the progressive response to the crisis will depend on the ability of movements around the world not only to rise to the challenge of the socio-economic and environmental problems that plague our world but also to respond to the campaigns of the intolerant who will use these problems to promote false solutions based on hate and scapegoating. In many parts of the world today, the walls of hate are going up in the form of anti-immigrant sentiment and religious fundamentalism.

The descent into xenophobia, cynicism, and anxiety in many countries has been vastly exacerbated by the effects of the economic crisis. But that descent began long before the crash. For the past quarter-century, mainstream political parties of all shades have utterly failed to cope with the widening gap in income and wealth between a small segment of the population that has been enormously enriched and the vast majority of the population of the advanced countries and, much more so, the population of humanity as a whole. The economic collapse has made the failure to address the problem of the widening wealth and income gaps even more urgent. The boiling anger of those who are shut off from the possibility of advance can open the door to an advance for progressive politics, but it can also feed into the agenda of those who fabricate lies that the world is run by some ethnic or religious group that can be isolated and attacked.

For the Nazis, the theory was that the world was run by Jewish financiers who had stabbed Germany in the back during the First World War. Today the world is plagued by new concerns that are used to marginalize people: in Europe there is fear of Muslim immigrants and their descendants; in America there is fear of Hispanic immigrants; and in many parts of the world there is propaganda from religious fundamentalists who seek to blame ills on people of other faiths. These forms of hatred can be used to tell people that immigrants are taking jobs away from the French, that newcomers are robbing the U.S. middle class of its standard of living, or that God has a divine plan for people of particular faiths that must not be thwarted by the designs of others.

While exclusionism is omni-present, so too are the progressives. Even before the crash—and now continuing after its onset—a wide range of progressive movements had been putting the case for a new economics that would serve humanity and safeguard the planet against environmental ruin. These movements are diverse, pluralist, and democratic. From among them come the voices of social democrats, socialists, liberals, humanists, environmentalists, non-fundamentalist religious believers, feminists, trade unionists, urban activists, anti-poverty organizations, students, and writers. A new politics of the planet has been taking shape. Its philosophical origins are both ancient and contemporary. This politics of the planet takes unique forms in each country, arising out of particular cultures and conditions.

The broad challenge is to reinvigorate democracy at the local and national levels, while advancing programs that for the first time in history are in keeping with the interests of people everywhere. The perspective has to be planetary. But unlike the corporate agenda that has stripped away effective power from the level of the nation-state, and from working people, the progressive agenda needs to return effective power to nations so that they can design their social systems, govern their own economies, and act as stewards for their share of the planet.

If this sort of agenda sounds as though it is alive with paradox and contradiction, it is—and it is the reverse of much that has driven the global agenda of the past three decades, during the so-called age of globalization. Globalization has, in truth, drawn all people and all nations into a closer set of relationships with one another, and those connections have been based on amplifying the power of the few at the expense of the many on a wide range of fronts. Globalization has effectively paralyzed democracy to an alarming extent.

While its proponents have claimed that globalization has opened borders and reduced the power of the state, the phenomenon has, rather, only opened borders to the flow of capital while reducing the power of most of the states of the world, leaving the socio-economic future to be shaped by a handful of states (the United States most important among them). In the process borders have been closed to most of humanity.

A case in point is the plight of desperate people who take to flimsy vessels to sail from Africa to Europe, all too often dying during the voyage, in the hope that they will be able to make a living in Europe for themselves and their families. Similarly, tens of thousands of Mexicans take their lives in their hands each year to attempt to make it past the growing army of border guards into the United States, where they can work for low pay and with no job protection to make a living in a country in which the political rhetoric has increasingly reduced these migrants to the status of pariahs. The U.S. economy would be hard-pressed to function without these illegal immigrants, but on the political right the harsh standard is for politicians to advocate the denial of all social and educational benefits to these workers and their children. Across the developed world, the barriers are going up to stop desperate economic refugees from reaching the promised land.

The democratic agenda needs to regard this staggering inequality as the most important matter to be addressed; and unless it is effectively addressed, little else that is achieved will matter very much.

Putting the world on the road towards equality will call for as much creative energy as the great democratic upheavals of the eighteenth century. Power needs to be returned to nation-states so that their citizens can both address inequality within their own countries and establish an agenda to address the inequality between nations. Such a power shift can only be achieved through the mobilization of the democratic energies of a wide spectrum of the population.

The issue on which this majority can be mobilized is easily located: it is the economic treadmill on which the majority of people in the developed world find themselves. Wage and salary earners are on an economic treadmill. On average their living standards have not risen for the past several decades, and they are increasingly plunging into debt to finance the purchase of homes and send their children to post-secondary educational institutions whose tuition has been skyrocketing. The huge economic gains of this period have gone only to a few. For instance, twenty years ago the remuneration of a top U.S. corporate manager was forty times that of a typical employee. Now typically the top manager makes one hundred and ten times as much.

Wage and salary earners are increasingly conscious of the emergence of levels of inequality that have not been seen since the aristocratic age that preceded the American and French revolutions. Those at the helm of the advanced economies tout the idea of "flexibility," the notion that the investment of capital and the location of enterprises should be directed by the marketplace to wherever in the world they can be most effective. For instance, one respected voice representing this point of view is *The Economist* weekly magazine in London. On January 20, 2007, *The Economist* proclaimed, "These are the glory days of global capitalism. . . . This newspaper has long argued that a mobile society is better than an equal one."

I would argue—and many with the point of view of *The Economist* will stoutly disagree—that inequality has gone too far to be compatible with a vigorous democracy.

Returning a good deal of effective economic sovereignty to nation-states does not mean erecting economic walls around countries. That is neither desirable nor possible in our age. Instead, what it means, above all, is a shift in the control of capital from the ever larger financial holdings that now exist to local, regional, or national holdings. What drove the world to the yawning inequality of the neo-liberal age and then to the crash and the economic cataclysm that followed was the existence of ever larger pools of capital controlled privately. The control of capital has always been at the centre of capitalism; and those who control capital have always had the whip hand. During the neo-liberal age, the use of capital was increasingly delinked from the expansion of productive capacity. Instead, in the mega-extension of the financial sector, especially in the United States, the investment of capital through a wide range of financial instruments was increasingly used to siphon profits out of the bubble economies that developed first in the dot.coms and then in housing. Financial-sector parasitism was the consequence of neo-liberalism and a central cause of the crash.

Progressive advance means setting things the right way up in the economy so that the people at large become the masters of capital and not the other way around. Placing pools of capital in local, regional, and national holdings and democratizing both the control of capital and of the workplace need to be the next great chapter in the history of democracy. There is, to be sure, no easy fit between this step and the one that needs to accompany it—the establishment of a much more equitable relationship between the wealthy and the poor countries of the world.

Will advantageously placed nations use their privileged positions to ensure more for themselves than for those with whom they conduct commerce in poorer countries? The short answer is yes, certainly. But in a world with capital pools divided up into local, regional, and national holdings, the balance of power could effectively shift towards a new, democratic political coalition of both rich and poor countries. A politics of local, national, and global development, dedicated towards more egalitarian outcomes and sustainable environmental policies, could emerge.

The neo-liberal system has fallen into pieces and cannot be put together again. Nor should humanity attempt it. It is time to move on to a better future.

CHAPTER TWO — ONSET OF THE CRASH

1   ABC News, Sept. 15, 2008.
2   *The New York Times*, Sept. 16, 2008.
3   John Kenneth Galbraith, *The Great Crash, 1919* (New York: Houghton Mifflin, 1997), p.1.
4   *The New York Times*, Dec. 21, 2008.
5   Ibid.
6   Ibid.
7   *International Herald Tribune*, Oct. 10, 2008.
8   *The New York Times*, March 29, 2007.
9   *The New York Times*, Jan. 9, 2009.
10 *The Guardian* (London), Jan. 9, 2009.
11 Ibid.; *The Economist*, May 2, 2009.
12 *The Toronto Star*, Jan. 10, 2009.
13 *Calgary Herald*, Jan. 10, 2009.
14 *The Globe and Mail*, Feb. 6, 2009.
15 *The Economist*, May 2, 2009.
16 George Soros, *The Crash of 2008 and What It Means: The New Paradigm for Financial Markets* (New York: PublicAffairs, 2009), p.83.

CHAPTER THREE — THE LIFE AND TIMES OF SPECULATIVE BUBBLES

1 Galbraith, *Great Crash*, p.6.
2 Ibid.
3 *International Herald Tribune*, Jan. 26, 2009.

CHAPTER FOUR — THE HOUSING BUBBLE

1 *The New York Times*, Dec. 21, 2008.
2 Ibid.
3 Ibid.
4 *The New York Times*, Dec. 19, 2008.
5 Ibid.

CHAPTER FIVE — THE PERILS OF DEFLATION

1 *The Guardian*, May 19, 2009.
2 *Financial Post*, May 20, 2009.
3 *Calgary Herald*, May 20, 2009.
4 *Financial Post*, May 6, 2009.
5 *The Globe and Mail*, July 24, 2009; CBC.ca, July 23, 2009.
6 Inflationdata.com.
7 *The New York Times*, Sept. 7, 2008.

**CHAPTER SIX — INCOME AND WEALTH INEQUALITY:
AN UNDERLYING CAUSE OF THE CRASH**

1 Statistics Canada, *Canada Year Book 1978-79* (Hull, Quebec: Supply and Services Canada, 1978), p.267.
2 National Center for Educational Statistics, 2008.
3 Center on Budget and Policy Priorities, Aug. 26, 2008.
4 Ellen Russell and Mathieu Dufour, "Rising Profit Shares, Falling Wage Shares," Canadian Centre for Policy Alternatives, Ottawa, June 2007.
5 U.S. Census Bureau, *Statistical Abstract of the United States: 2008*, 127th ed. (Washington, D.C., 2007), p.423; Human Resources and Skills Development Canada, Ottawa, Statistics Canada, 2008 (Cat. No. 71F0004XCB).

CHAPTER SEVEN − AMERICAN DEBT AND THE GLOBAL CRISIS

1 General Accounting Office, Financial Audit: Bureau of the Public Debt's Fiscal Years, Washington, D.C., 2008 and 2007.
2 *The New York Times*, March 25, 2009.
3 *The Economist*, May 2, 2009. The current account includes the trade in commodities, tourism, and the trade in services, including profits, dividends, and interest payments between the United States and all other countries over the course of a year.
4 *The New York Times*, Jan. 30, 2009.
5 Ibid.
6 Kevin Phillips, *Bad Money: Reckless Finance, Failed Politics, and the Global Crisis of American Capitalism* (New York: Penguin Books, 2008, 2009), pp.xvi, xvii, xviii.
7 Ibid., p.xviii.
8 Ibid., p.xvi.
9 *The New York Times*, March 27, 2009.
10 Phillips, *Bad Money*, p.xxviii.
11 Ibid., p.xxvi.
12 *The New York Times*, Feb. 2, 2009.
13 *The New York Times*, Feb. 1, 2009.
14 *The New York Times*, Feb. 2, 2009.

CHAPTER EIGHT − THE HOUSE THE NEO-LIBERALS BUILT

1 A.N. Wilson, *After the Victorians: The World Our Parents Knew* (London: Arrow Books, 2006), pp.509–12.
2 John Kenneth Galbraith, *The New Industrial State* (Princeton, N.J.: The James Madison Library in American Politics, Princeton University Press, 2007).
3 John Maynard Keynes, *The General Theory of Employment, Interest and Money* (London: Houghton Mifflin Harcourt, 2001); Keynes, *The Economic Consequences of the Peace* (London: Dover Publications, 2004).
4 Charles Murray, *Losing Ground: American Social Policy, 1950–1980* (New York: Basic Books, 1994).
5 F.A. Hayek, *The Road to Serfdom* (London: University of Chicago Press, 2007).
6 The real rate of return on a bond is calculated by subtracting the rate of inflation from the nominal rate of interest on the bond. During some periods of

high inflation, there were actually negative rates of return on bonds because the rate of inflation exceeded the nominal rate of interest on the bond.

7   *The New York Times*, June 1, 2009.

8   Zbigniew Brzezinski, *The Grand Chessboard: American Primacy and Its Geostrategic Imperatives* (New York: Basic Books, 1997), p.198.

9   James Laxer, *The Perils of Empire: America and Its Imperial Predecessors* (Toronto: Viking Canada, 2008), p.222.

10   Ibid., pp.229, 230.

CHAPTER NINE – THE COMING GLOBAL ECONOMY

1   *The New York Times*, April 3, 2009.

2   VOA News.com, Feb. 2, 2009.

3   *Business Week*, April 20, 2009.

CHAPTER TEN – CANADA'S POLITICAL RESPONSE TO THE CRASH: AN EXERCISE IN DENIAL

1   Department of Finance, Canada, www.fin.gc.ca, Oct. 23, 2008.

2   *The Toronto Star*, June 4, 2009.

3   CBC News, Feb. 6, 2009.

4   Ibid.

CHAPTER ELEVEN – STAPLES, OIL SANDS, AND OTHER RESOURCEFUL FANTASIES

1   Harold Innis, *The Fur Trade in Canada* (Toronto: University of Toronto Press, 1999). The concluding chapter of this classic provides a clear overview of the staples thesis.

2   See R.T. Naylor, "The Rise and Fall of the Third Commercial Empire of the St. Lawrence," in *Capitalism and the National Question in Canada*, ed. Gary Teeple (Toronto: University of Toronto Press, 1972).

3   Stanley B. Ryerson, *Unequal Union: Confederation and the Roots of Conflict in the Canadas, 1815–1873* (Toronto: Progress Books, 1968), p.235.

4   W.A. Mackintosh, *The Economic Background of Dominion-Provincial Relations* (Toronto: Carleton Library, 1964), p.25.

5 See Vernon Fowke, *The National Policy and the Wheat Economy* (Toronto: University of Toronto Press, 1973).

6 Royal Ontario Nickel Commission, Report, 1917 (Toronto: Government of Ontario, 1917).

7 *The Globe and Mail*, July 13, 2009; Canadian Press, July 13, 2009.

8 Watkins Report: Task Force on Foreign Ownership and the Structure of Canadian Investment (Ottawa: Queen's Printer, 1968); Gray Report: Foreign Direct Investment in Canada (Ottawa: Queen's Printer, 1972).

9 James Laxer, *Oil and Gas: Ottawa, the Provinces and the Petroleum Industry* (Toronto: Lorimer, 1983), p.7.

10 James Laxer, *Canada's Energy Crisis* (Toronto: James Lorimer and Company, 1975), p.143.

11 James Laxer, *Oil* (Toronto: Groundwood Books, 2008), p.87.

12 Ibid., p.88.

13 Ibid., p.90.

14 Ibid., pp.91, 92.

15 Ibid., p.93.

16 *The Toronto Star*, April 28, 2009.

17 Laxer, *Oil*, pp.96, 97.

18 Andrew Nikiforuk, *Tar Sands: Dirty Oil and the Future of a Continent* (Vancouver: Greystone Books, 2008), pp.21, 22, 23.

19 Alberta Royalty Review Panel, May 24, 2007.

CHAPTER TWELVE — TRAINS, PLANES, AND AUTOMOBILES FOR TWENTY-FIRST-CENTURY CANADA

1 For a history of the development of transportation in Canada, see G.P. de T. Glazebrook, *A History of Transportation in Canada*, two vols. (Toronto: McClelland and Stewart, 1964).

2 For a history of the early decades of the Canadian automotive industry, see Royal Commission on the Automotive Industry, Appendix (Ottawa: Queen's Printer, 1961).

3 Dimitry Anastakis, "Between Nationalism and Continentalism: State Auto Industry Policy and the Canadian UAW, 1960–1970," *Labour*, Spring 2004.

4 John Holmes, "The Auto Pact from 1965 to the CUSFTA," in *The Auto Pact: Investment, Labour and the WTO*, ed. Maureen Irish (The Hague/London/

New York: Kluwer Law International, 2003), p.17.

5 Irish, ed., *Auto Pact*, p.ix.

6 Japan Automobile Manufacturers Association (JAMA) Canada, *2006 Annual Review*, Toronto, pp.3, 6, 4.

7 Reuters, Nov. 19, 2008.

8 *Wall Street Journal*, March 30, 2009.

9 Associated Press, March 30, 2009.

10 *The Globe and Mail*, April 16, 2009.

11 *The Globe and Mail*, April 13, 2009.

12 Bloomberg news service, March 30, 2009.

13 Reuters, April 30, 2009.

14 *U.S. News and World Report*, May 1, 2009.

15 Ibid.

16 *Financial Post*, June 1, 2009.

17 *The Toronto Star*, June 1, 2009.

18 *The Toronto Star*, June 3, 2009.

19 Ibid.

20 Monte Paulsen, "Off the Rails: How Canada Fell from Leader to Laggard in High-Speed Rail, and Why That Needs to Change," *The Walrus Magazine*, June 2009.

21 *The Toronto Star*, Feb. 25, 2009.

CHAPTER THIRTEEN — A PROGRESSIVE ECONOMIC STRATEGY FOR CANADA

1 CBC News, Oct. 10, 2008.

2 Canwest News Service, Nov. 12, 2008.

3 *The Toronto Star*, April 23, 2009.

CHAPTER FOURTEEN — ECONOMICS FOR HUMANITY

1 *The New York Times*, April 18, 2009.

2 Ibid.

3 *The New York Times*, March 18, 2009.

4 Jacques Attali, *La crise, et après* (Paris: Fayard, 2009), pp.16, 17.

emigration from, 147; empires and, 214–15; energy megaprojects, 163–64; as energy superpower, 20, 167; environmental policy, 168; exports, 121, 141–42, 146, 148–50, 154, 157, 158–61, 166–67, 171–73, 177–78, 181, 185, 204, 215, 217, 218; federal budget (2009), 133–38; federal election: (1974) 161; (1979) 162; (1980) 162; (1984), 165; (2008), 127, 129, 210; financial institutions, 128, 131; Foreign Investment Revenue Agency (FIRA), 165; highway construction, 174; home ownership, 41; housing prices, 44; immigration to, 147; imports, 134, 147–48, 157, 166, 178–79, 181; income inequality, 54–55, 62; indebtedness of, 211; industrialization, 148; infrastructure spending, 135; Liberal-NDP coalition, 132–33, 135–36, 138; Liberal Party, 19, 128–29, 132–33, 135–38, 147, 171, 172, 201, 215; manufacturing sector, 137, 141, 148, 151, 154, 156–57, 170–71, 176, 215; media, 216; merchant-banker class, 145–46; National Energy Board, 160–61; National Energy Program (NEP), 162, 164–65; National Policy, 147–48, 157, 196; New Democratic Party (NDP), 128, 132–33, 135, 138, 161, 215; Petroleum Incentive Program (PIP), 163, 166; petroleum price regime, 160–61, 163, 166; postwar recovery of, 96; primary commodity production, 141–42, 146, 148, 149, 154, 156–59, 171–72; progressive economic strategy for, 207–19; pro-

rogation, 132–33; public service, 57; publishing industry, 170; railways, 173, 175, 195–201, 203, 214; rebellions (1837–38), 144; recession, 18, 46–47, 131, 134, 147; response of to 2008 crash, 127–39; right wing, 48–50; tax cuts, 128, 134; trade surplus of with U.S., 107, 157, 182; trade with U.K., 217; trade with U.S., 179–81, 217; transcontinental railway, 147; transportation industry, 173–206; unemployment, 18–20, 137–38; United States and, 71, 130, 157, 208, 216–17; universal health-care system, 92; "wealth effect," 41; welfare state, 92

Canada Mortgage and Housing Corporation (CMHC), 210
Canada–U.S. Auto Pact, 159, 180–84, 194
Canada–U.S. Free Trade Agreement (FTA), 165–67, 180, 184, 194
Canadian Auto Workers (CAW), 188–90, 213
Canadian Broadcasting Corporation (CBC), 216
Canadian Centre for Policy Alternatives, 54
Canadian Copper Company, 150
Canadian National Railways (CNR), 196, 197–98, 214
Canadian Pacific Railway (CPR), 147, 195–96, 198
"Canadian Value Added," 181
Cape Coral (Florida), 27
capital: control of, 234; empowerment of control over, 227; as foundation of economy, 224; free movement of, 61;